I0886274

# SKILL SHARPENERS Math 1

Keep Your Child's Academic Skills Sharp

This book belongs to

name

# Contents

# How to Use This Book

## Practicing Math Skills

Math is in the world around us. Children start to notice how many there are of something when they are quite young, especially if someone else has more! They also notice that quantities change as objects are received, given away, or used. Studies show that children develop math sense and reasoning best through making connections between objects and written numbers. This book will help your child connect real objects and situations with math language and operations.

### Use of Manipulatives

Using real-life objects to count, add, or subtract can help young children better understand math concepts. Drawing the objects can also be helpful. As your child completes the activities in this book, provide him or her with objects to use to help work out each math item. Game pieces, silverware, paper clips—any objects around the house will work. Once children become comfortable with counting, adding, and subtracting, they will probably no longer need the real-life objects to help them calculate.

### Counting, Adding, and Subtracting Activities

Provide support as your child works through counting, addition, and subtraction items. Read the directions to your child. If there is an example at the top of the page, explain it to your child. Next, to verify understanding, have your child explain the example to you. Point to any math symbols on the page and ask your child what they mean. Explain any math symbols that your child is not sure of. If your child struggles with problems that are not illustrated, have your child draw, use manipulatives, or act out the problem.

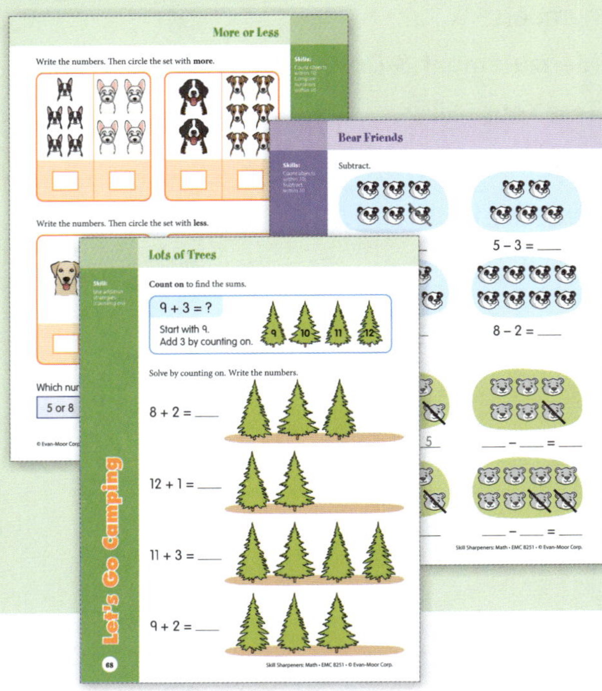

## Word Problems

Word problems help relate math to real-life situations and develop reasoning skills. Read the word problem to your child if needed and make sure he or she understands all the words. Encourage your child to draw the situation; provide objects to represent the quantities. Give your child a chance to figure out the problem before you offer help. If your child is stuck or unsure how to proceed, use guiding questions such as, "What is the goal of the problem? What information do you have already? What do these numbers have to do with each other? Do you think you should add or subtract? Is there another number you need to figure out before you can find the answer?"

## Other Math Skills

Numbers are used to make graphs and measurements. Geometric shapes are explored and used to make patterns. Skip-counting creates dot-to-dot pictures. Different representations of time and money are matched. For these and other activities, read the directions to your child and make sure he or she understands the vocabulary. Allow enough time for your child to solve the problem or complete the task. If he or she is unable to, suggest strategies to try or provide other support.

# Number Words

**Skills:**
Write number words; Count objects within 10

Doggy Math

Write each number word.

| 0 | 1 | 2 | 3 | 4 | 5 |
|---|---|---|---|---|---|
| zero | one | two | three | four | five |
| 6 | 7 | 8 | 9 | 10 | |
| six | seven | eight | nine | ten | |

3 ____________ 2 ____________ 1 ____________

10 ____________ 9 ____________ 6 ____________

0 ____________ 4 ____________ 5 ____________

7 ____________ 8 ____________

Count. Draw a line to match.

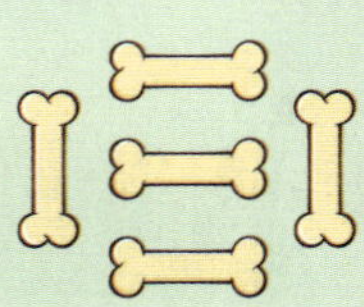 three

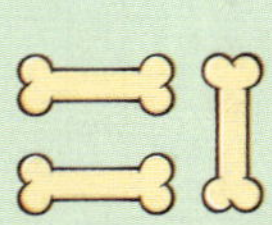 five

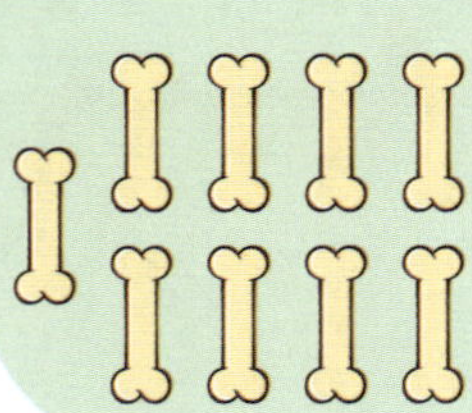 nine

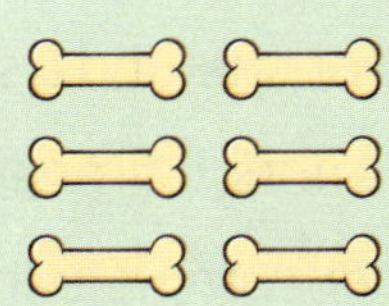 four

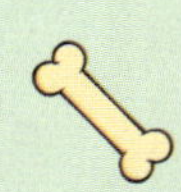 one

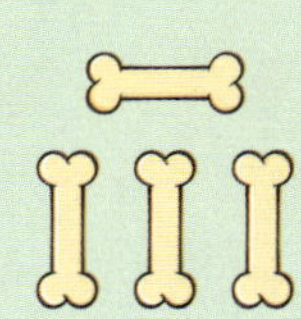 six

# Cute Pups

**Skill:**
Count objects within 10

Count the dogs. Circle the number.

0 1 2

1 2 3

0 1 2

3 4 5

4 5 6

2 3 4

3 4 5

4 5 6

2 3 4

# Find the Doghouse

**Skill:**
Count objects within 10

Doggy Math

Count. Draw lines to match the dogs to their houses.

# Doggy Bones

**Skills:**
Count objects within 10; Compare numbers within 10

Circle 7 bones.

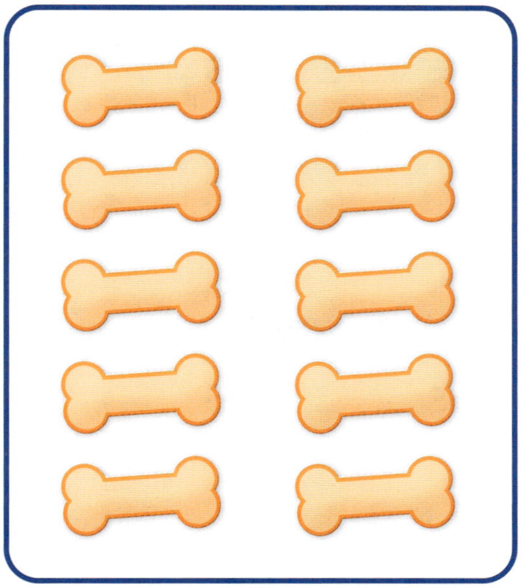

Circle 9 bones.

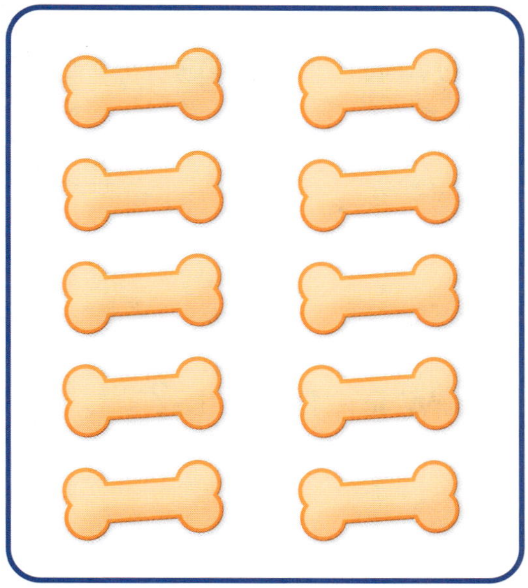

Draw 8 bones.

Draw 10 bones.

Circle the larger number on each bone.

# Count and Tell

**Skills:**
Count objects within 10; Compare numbers within 10

How many legs?  has _____ legs.

How many ears?  has _____ ears.

How many feet in all?
 and  have _____ feet in all.

How many bones? 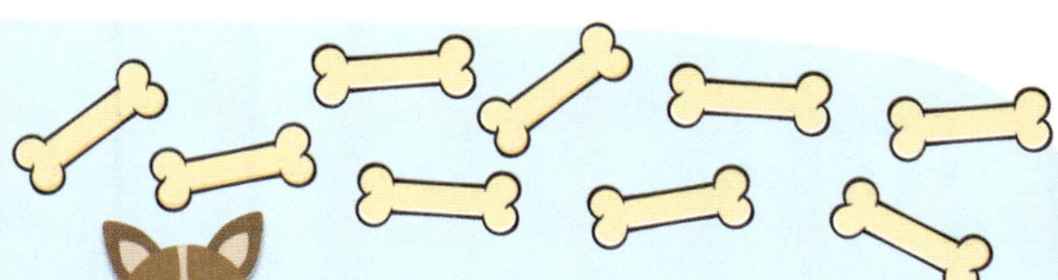
 has _____ bones.

Which answer is the largest? _____

Which answer is the smallest? _____

**Skills:**
Count objects within 10; Compare numbers within 10

Write the numbers. Then circle the set with **more**.

Write the numbers. Then circle the set with **less**.

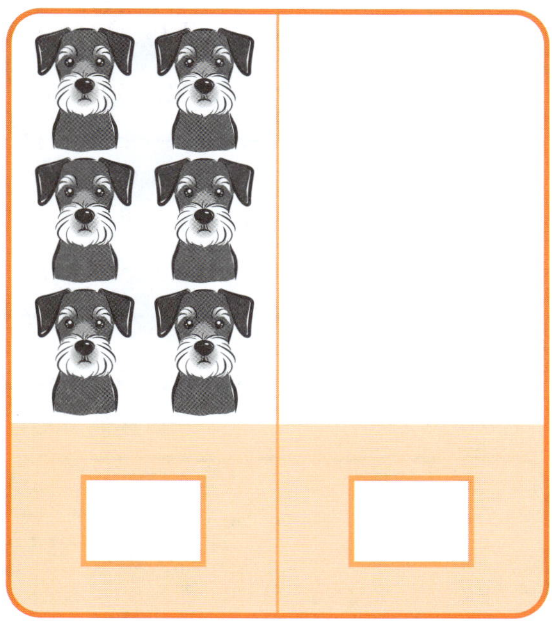

Which number is larger?

| 5 or 8 | 3 or 1 |
|---|---|

Which number is smaller?

| 7 or 2 | 9 or 0 |
|---|---|

# Making 6

**Skill:**
Add within 10

Write the numbers that show different ways you can make 6.

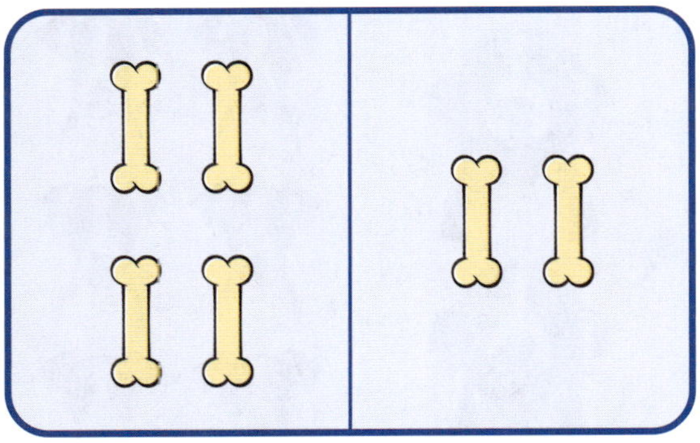

4 and 2

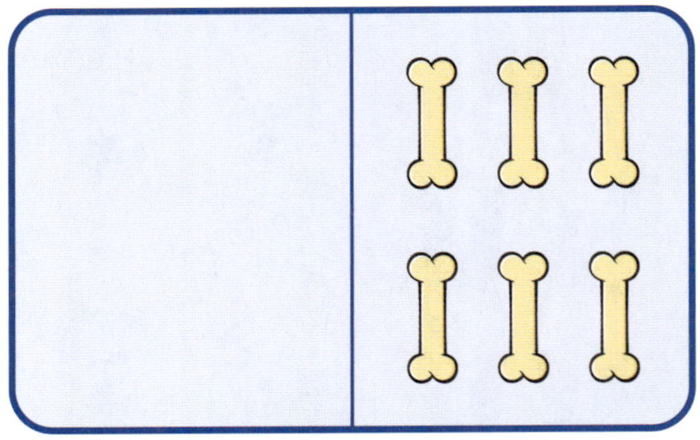

_____ and _____

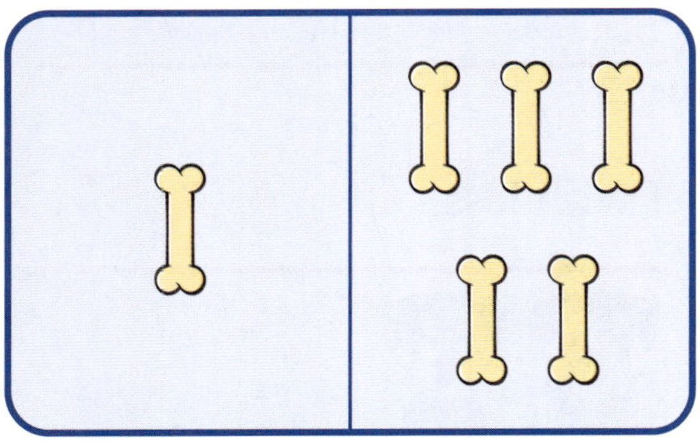

_____ and _____

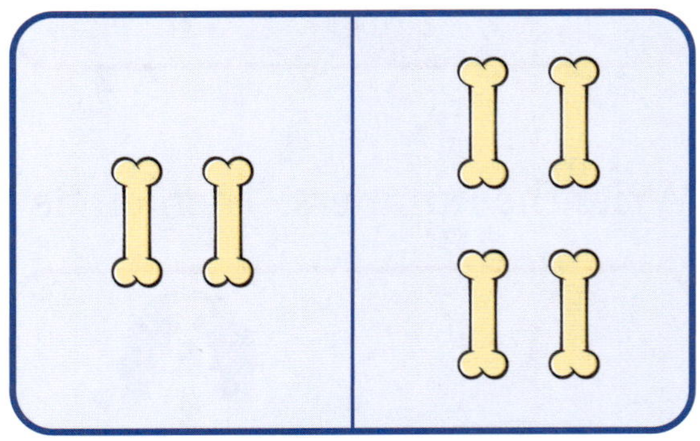

_____ and _____

Draw bones to show two other ways you can make 6.

_____ and _____

_____ and _____

Doggy Math

Draw the cans you need to make 7. Write the numbers.

**Skill:** Add within 10

5 and 2

_____ and _____

_____ and _____

_____ and _____

_____ and _____

_____ and _____

# Making 8

**Skill:**
Add within 10

Write the numbers that show different ways you can make 8.

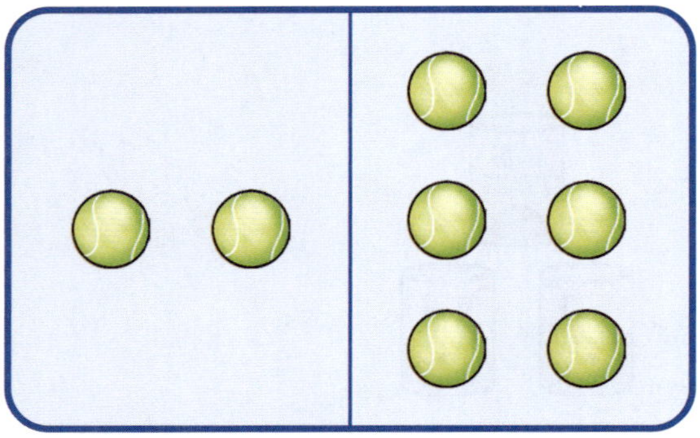

_____ and _____

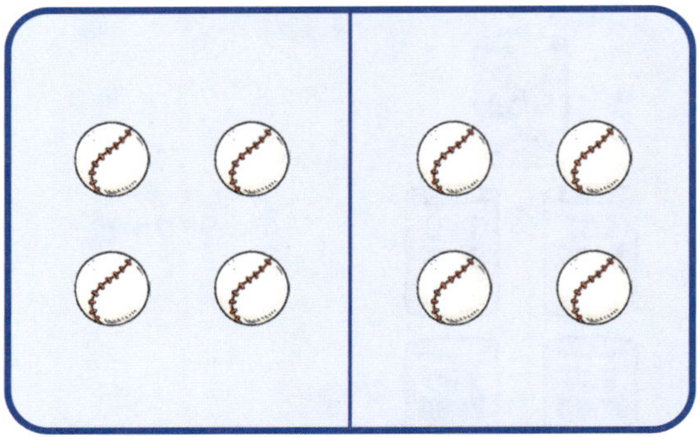

_____ and _____

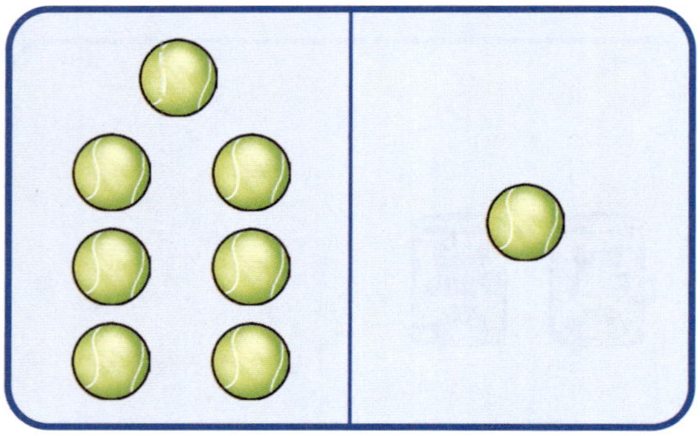

_____ and _____

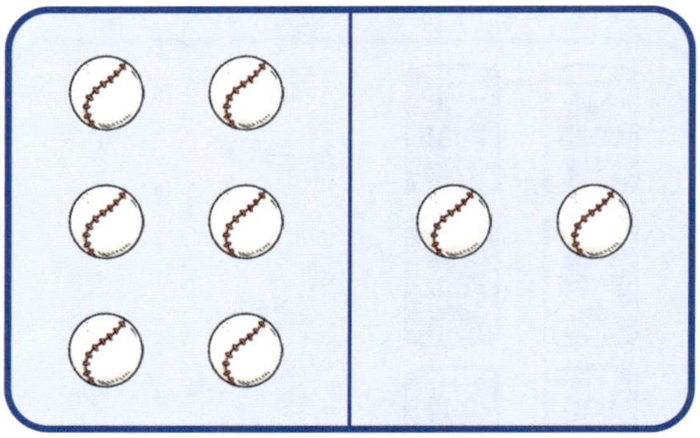

_____ and _____

Draw bones to show two other ways you can make 8.

_____ and _____

_____ and _____

# Dog Bone Measuring

**Skill:**
Measure length using nonstandard units

How long is each object?

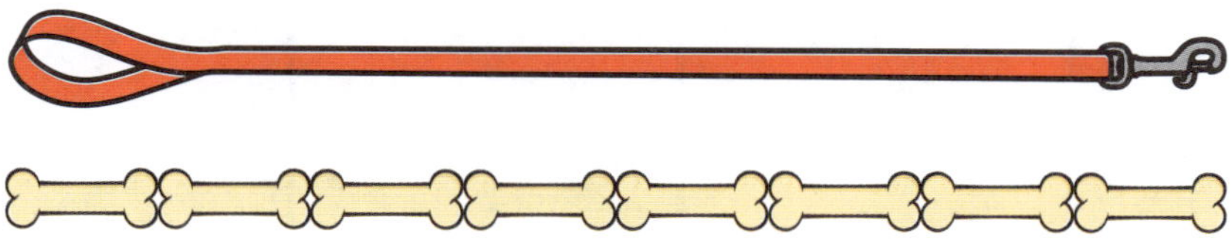

_______ 🦴

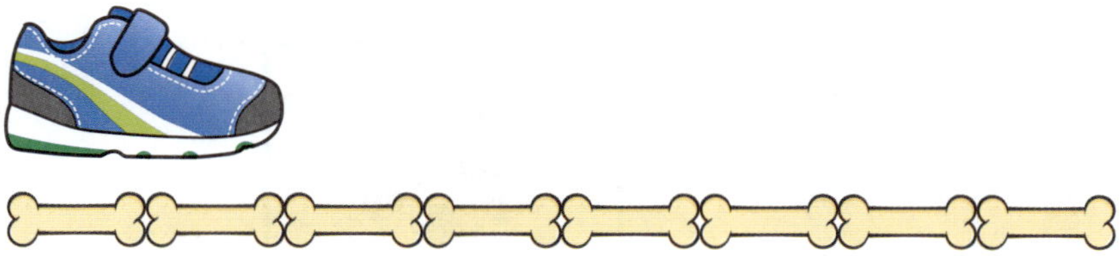

_______ 🦴

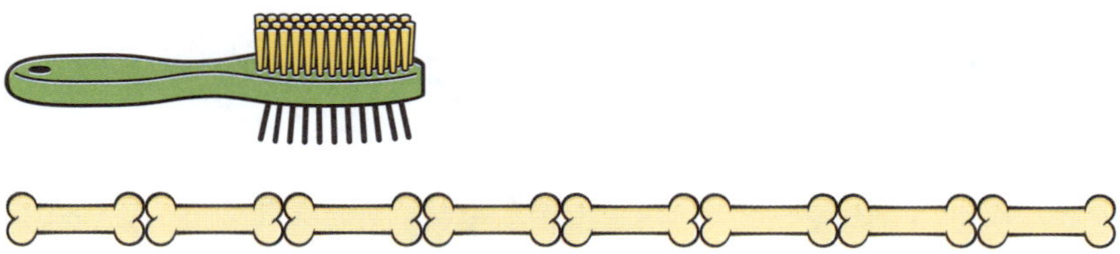

_______ 🦴

_______ 🦴

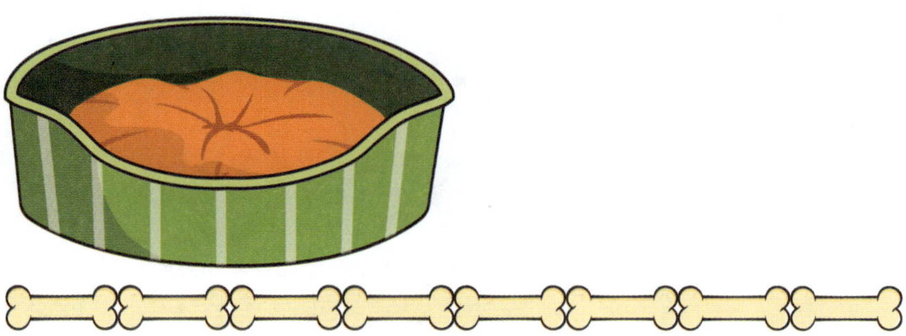

_______ 🦴

# The Pet Store

**Skill:**
Read a graph

Read the graph about a pet store. Answer the questions.

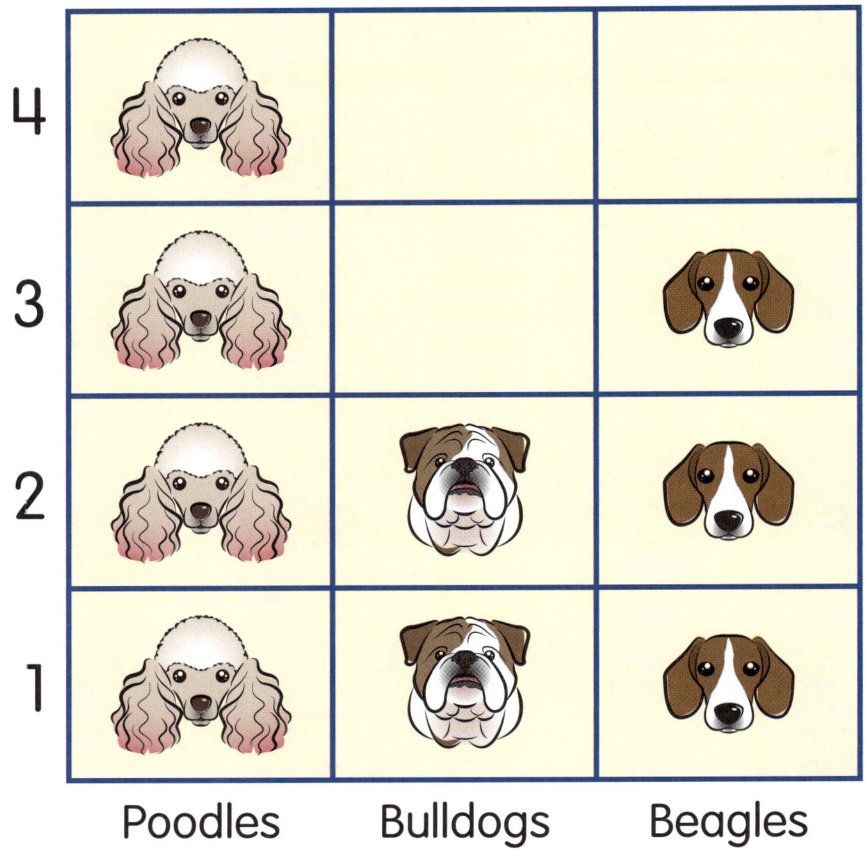


How many dogs are in the store?

 ______  ______  ______

How many dogs in all? ______

Are there more  or ?

The store has the most   .

TEST YOUR SKILLS

# Doggy Math

Count the dogs. Write the number to tell how many.

Fill in the circle to show how long it is.

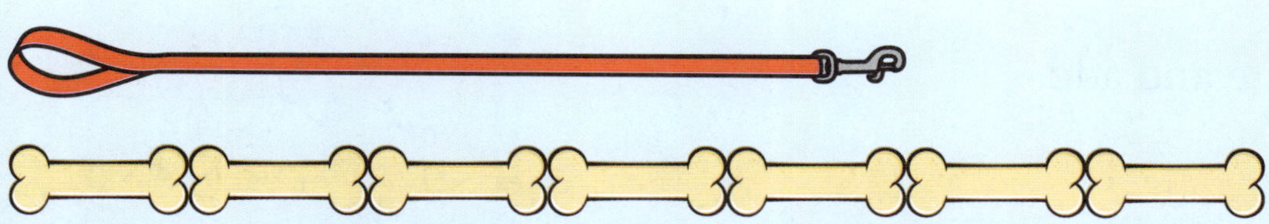

5 ○ 7 ○ 9 ○

Draw the cans you need to make 8. Write the numbers.

_____ and _____

# Let's Add Sheep

**Skills:**

Count objects within 10; Add within 10

On the Farm

Add.

1 + 2 = ____

3 + 1 = ____

1 + 4 = ____

6 + 0 = ____

Write and add.

__1__ + __1__ = __2__

____ + ____ = ____

____ + ____ = ____

____ + ____ = ____

# Animals on the Farm

**Skills:**
Solve word problems; Add within 10

Add.

There are 2 horses.
2 more horses come.
How many horses now?

2 + 2 = 4

4 horses

There are 3 sheep.
3 more sheep come.
How many sheep now?

____ + ____ = ____

☐ sheep

There are 0 hens.
5 hens come.
How many hens now?

____ + ____ = ____

☐ hens

There are 2 goats.
1 more goat comes.
How many goats now?

____ + ____ = ____

☐ goats

# Playful Sheep

**Skill:**
Add within 10

On the Farm

Add.

2 + 2 = ____ 3 + 2 = ____ 4 + 2 = ____

1 + 2 = ____ 0 + 2 = ____ 1 + 1 = ____

3 + 1 = ____ 1 + 0 = ____ 0 + 3 = ____

0 + 0 = ____ 2 + 3 = ____ 3 + 3 = ____

| 3 | 2 | 0 | 3 | 0 |
|---|---|---|---|---|
| + 1 | + 3 | + 3 | + 3 | + 0 |
| ☐ | ☐ | ☐ | ☐ | ☐ |

| 1 | 4 | 4 | 2 | 1 |
|---|---|---|---|---|
| + 0 | + 2 | + 1 | + 2 | + 1 |
| ☐ | ☐ | ☐ | ☐ | ☐ |

**Skill:**
Use properties of addition (commutative)

# The Answer Is the Same

Add.

| | | |
|---|---|---|
| 3 + 2 = ____<br>2 + 3 = ____ | 0 + 1 = ____<br>1 + 0 = ____ | 1 + 2 = ____<br>2 + 1 = ____ |
| 0 + 4 = ____<br>4 + 0 = ____ | 1 + 5 = ____<br>5 + 1 = ____ | 0 + 6 = ____<br>6 + 0 = ____ |
| 3 + 0 = ____<br>0 + 3 = ____ | 3 + 1 = ____<br>1 + 3 = ____ | 4 + 2 = ____<br>2 + 4 = ____ |

Write two addition problems for each cow.

**EXAMPLE**

1 + 2 = 3

2 + 1 = 3

| 2, 3, 5 | 1, 5, 6 |
|---|---|
| ____ + ____ = ____ | ____ + ____ = ____ |
| ____ + ____ = ____ | ____ + ____ = ____ |

# How Many Chicks?

**Skill:** Subtract within 10

On the Farm

Subtract.

3 – 2 = 1

5 – 3 = ____

4 – 0 = ____

6 – 4 = ____

Write and subtract.

5 – 1 = 4

____ – ____ = ____

____ – ____ = ____

____ – ____ = ____

# Animals Go Away

Subtract.

There are 5 hens.
1 hen goes away.
How many hens now?

____ − ____ = ____

hens

There are 4 cows.
2 cows go away.
How many cows now?

____ − ____ = ____

cows

There are 6 chicks.
2 chicks go away.
How many chicks now?

____ − ____ = ____

chicks

There are 5 horses.
3 horses go away.
How many horses now?

____ − ____ = ____

horses

**Skills:**
Solve word problems; Subtract within 10

# Swim Time

**Skill:**
Subtract within 10

On the Farm

Subtract.

5 – 5 = ____ 2 – 1 = ____ 6 – 5 = ____

3 – 1 = ____ 0 – 0 = ____ 4 – 3 = ____

6 – 6 = ____ 5 – 2 = ____ 3 – 0 = ____

5 – 0 = ____ 6 – 2 = ____ 1 – 1 = ____

| 5 | 2 | 4 | 5 | 1 |
|---|---|---|---|---|
| – 5 | – 1 | – 3 | – 5 | – 0 |
| ☐ | ☐ | ☐ | ☐ | ☐ |

| 6 | 5 | 3 | 5 | 3 |
|---|---|---|---|---|
| – 3 | – 2 | – 0 | – 4 | – 1 |
| ☐ | ☐ | ☐ | ☐ | ☐ |

# Farmer Mac's House

**Skill:**
Identify two-dimensional shapes

Color the shapes.

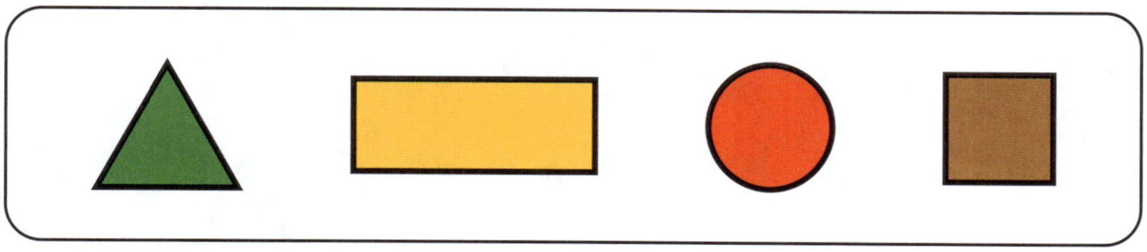

Count each shape. Write how many.

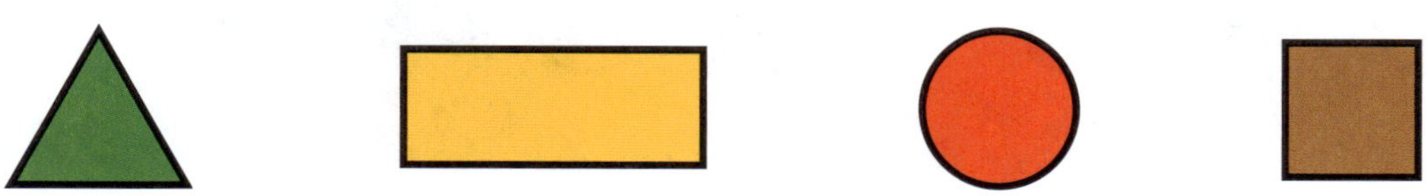

_____ _____ _____ _____

# Look Both Ways

**Skill:**
Identify two-dimensional shapes

Solve the riddle. Write the matching letter above the shape.

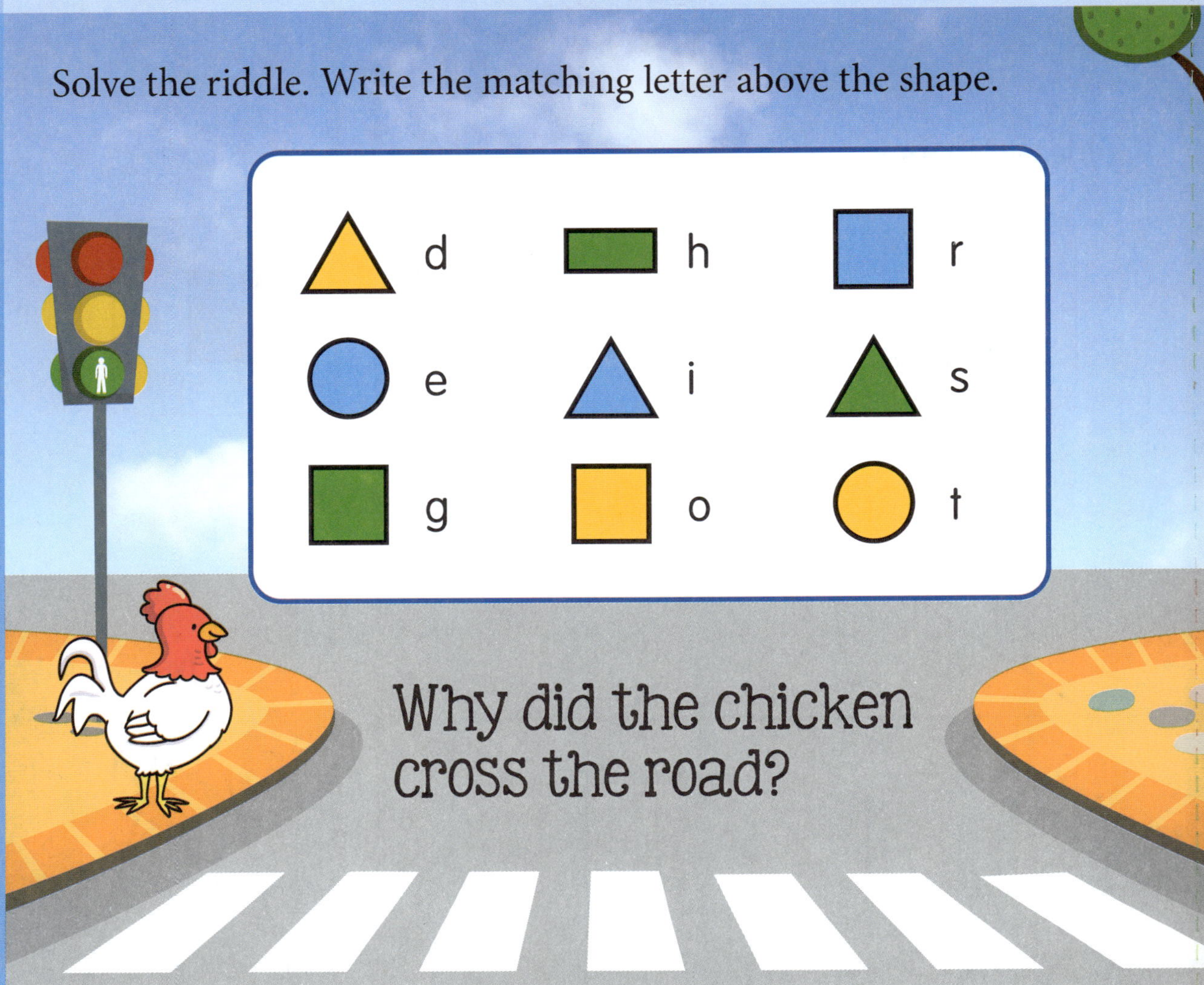


Why did the chicken cross the road?

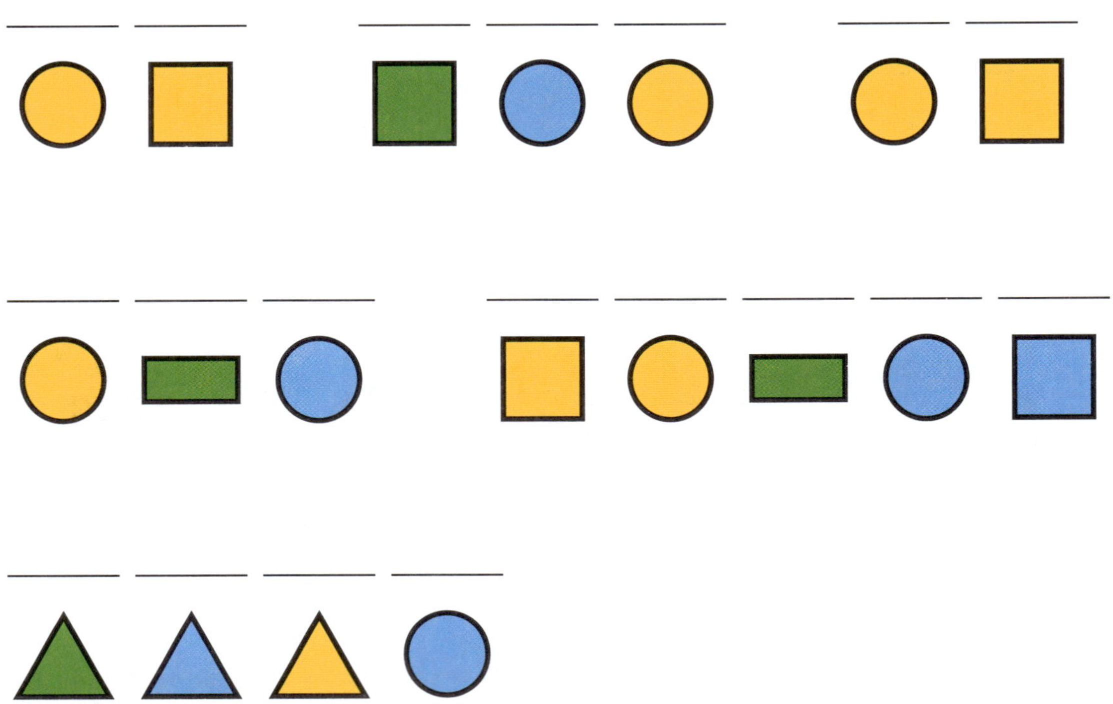

On the Farm

**Skills:**
Count objects within 10; Interpret a diagram

Write how many.

 in the ◯? _____

 in the ☐? _____

 in both the ◯ and the ☐? _____

 in both the ◯ and the ☐? _____

 in the ☐ but **not** in the ◯? _____

TEST YOUR SKILLS

On the Farm

Add.

3 + 3 = ____     1 + 2 = ____     2 + 3 = ____

Subtract.

4 − 1 = ____     6 − 2 = ____     6 − 6 = ____

Color the shapes.

Read and answer.

There are 3  in the mud. 2 more  come.

How many  are in the mud now? ____ 

**Skill:** Add within 10

Add.

7 + 1 = ____

3 + 4 = ____

1 + 6 = ____

5 + 3 = ____

Write and add.

____ + ____ = ____

____ + ____ = ____

____ + ____ = ____

____ + ____ = ____

# Teddy Bear Colors

Note: You may need to help your child read the word problems.

**Skills:**
Solve word problems; Add within 10

Fun with Bears

Add.

4 bears are brown.
4 bears are white.
How many bears in all?

____ + ____ = ____

☐ bears

2 bears are red.
4 bears are blue.
How many bears in all?

____ + ____ = ____

☐ bears

6 bears are green.
2 bears are yellow.
How many bears in all?

____ + ____ = ____

☐ bears

4 bears are purple.
3 bears are orange.
How many bears in all?

____ + ____ = ____

☐ bears

Skill:
Compare numbers within 10

Write **>** to show **greater than**. Write **<** to show **less than**.

$3 > 2$

The number of bears is **greater than** the number of fish.

$2 < 3$

The number of bears is **less than** the number of fish.

1 ◯ 5

7 ◯ 6

8 ◯ 4

2 ◯ 4

6 ◯ 7

4 ◯ 5

# Bear Friends

**Skills:**

Count objects within 10; Subtract within 10

Subtract.

6 – 1 = 5

5 – 3 = ____

7 – 5 = ____

8 – 2 = ____

Write and subtract.

7 – 2 = 5

____ – ____ = ____

____ – ____ = ____

____ – ____ = ____

Fun with Bears

# Hungry Bears

**Skills:**
Solve word problems; Subtract within 10

Read. Write the problems. Solve them.

Black Bear had 7 berries. He ate 3 berries.

How many berries were left?

$$\begin{array}{r} 7 \\ -\,3 \\ \hline 4 \end{array}$$

4 berries were left.

6 baby bears were in a tree. 1 climbed down.

How many baby bears were still in the tree?

_____ baby bears were still in the tree.

Grizzly Bear caught 8 fish. 1 swam away.

How many fish were left?

_____ fish were left.

Sun Bear had 7 nuts. Sun Bear ate 5 of them.

How many nuts were left?

_____ nuts were left.

# Color the Bear

**Skill:**
Subtract within 10

Subtract. Color.

| orange | brown | blue | red |
|---|---|---|---|
| 0 | 1 | 2 | 3 |

| green | purple | yellow |
|---|---|---|
| 4 | 5 | 6 |

Subtract.

6 – 6 = ____ 3 – 3 = ____ 4 – 4 = ____

8 – 8 = ____ 5 – 5 = ____ 2 – 2 = ____

When you subtract a number from itself, you get ____.

Fun with Bears

**Skill:**
Add and subtract within 10

# Bears at Play

Add.

$2 + 3 =$ ____ $4 + 4 =$ ____ $6 + 1 =$ ____

$4 + 2 =$ ____ $2 + 5 =$ ____ $5 + 3 =$ ____

Subtract.

$6 - 6 =$ ____ $8 - 1 =$ ____ $7 - 5 =$ ____

$5 - 3 =$ ____ $7 - 3 =$ ____ $8 - 2 =$ ____

Add or subtract.

$\begin{array}{r} 3 \\ +3 \\ \hline \square \end{array}$ $\begin{array}{r} 6 \\ +2 \\ \hline \square \end{array}$ $\begin{array}{r} 5 \\ +0 \\ \hline \square \end{array}$ $\begin{array}{r} 4 \\ +3 \\ \hline \square \end{array}$ $\begin{array}{r} 2 \\ +6 \\ \hline \square \end{array}$

$\begin{array}{r} 6 \\ -2 \\ \hline \square \end{array}$ $\begin{array}{r} 7 \\ -1 \\ \hline \square \end{array}$ $\begin{array}{r} 8 \\ -8 \\ \hline \square \end{array}$ $\begin{array}{r} 5 \\ -2 \\ \hline \square \end{array}$ $\begin{array}{r} 8 \\ -6 \\ \hline \square \end{array}$

Fun with Bears

# In the Woods

**Skill:**
Measure length using inches

How many inches?

The berry is _____ inch wide.

The hive is _____ inches wide.

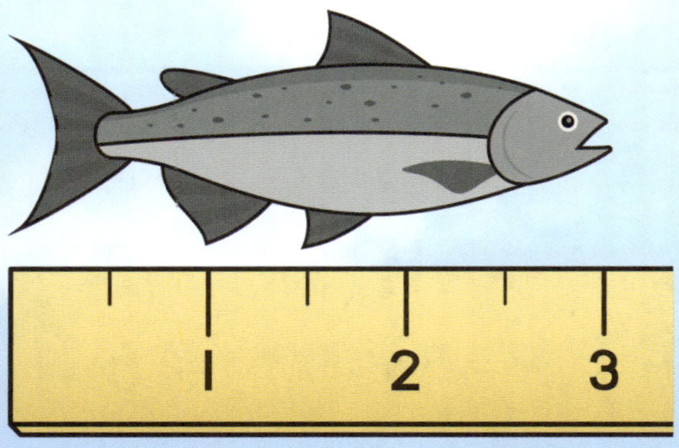


The fish is _____ inches long.

The flower is _____ inch wide.

The baby bear is _____ inches long.

**Skill:**
Read a graph

Read the graph. Answer the questions.

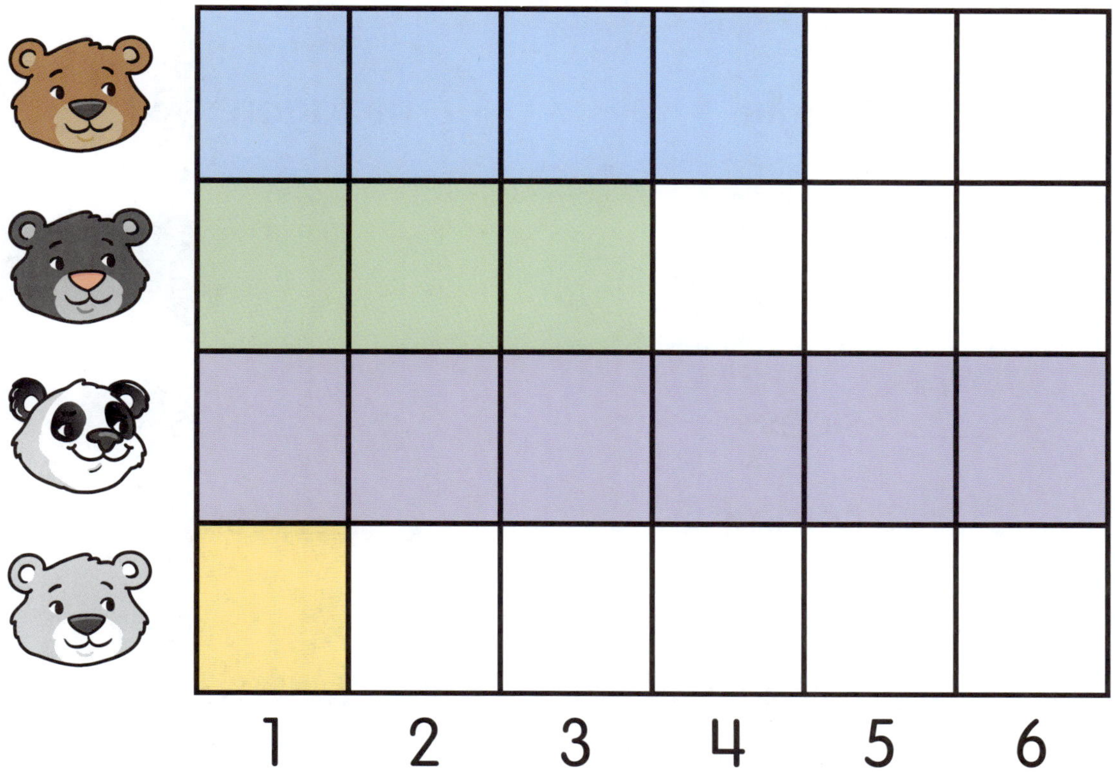

How many ? _____

How many ? _____

How many more  than ? _____ more

How many more  than ? _____ more

How many more  than ? _____ more

# Corners and Sides

**Skill:**
Identify attributes of shapes

Count the number of sides and corners.
Write the numbers.

**rectangle**

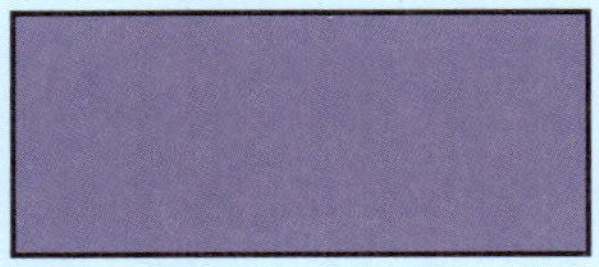

4 sides

4 corners

**hexagon**

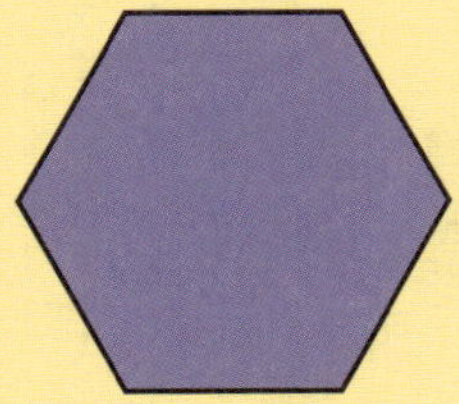

_____ sides

_____ corners

**pentagon**

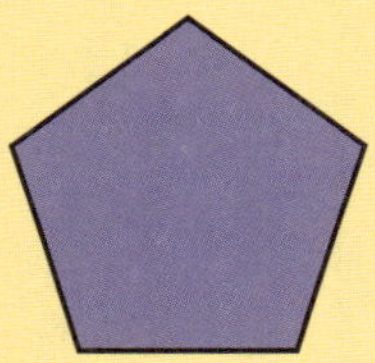

_____ sides

_____ corners

**circle**

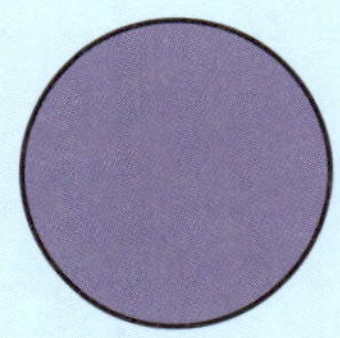

_____ sides

_____ corners

**square**

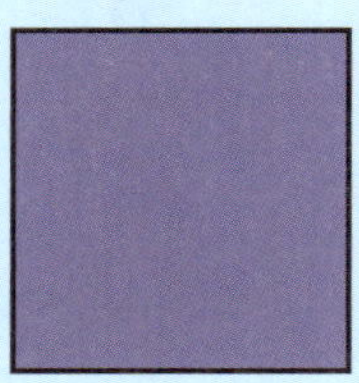

_____ sides

_____ corners

**triangle**

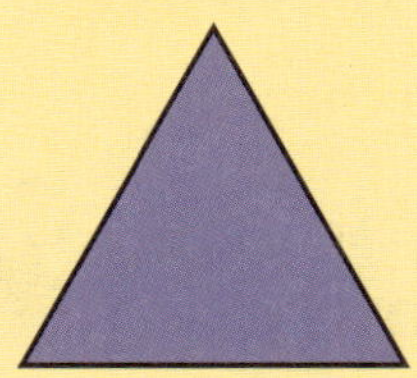

_____ sides

_____ corners

**Skill:** Identify attributes of shapes

Read how many sides and corners.
Draw the shapes.

| | |
|---|---|
| 4 sides<br>4 corners | 3 sides<br>3 corners |
| 4 equal sides<br>4 corners | 0 sides<br>0 corners |

Write to answer the questions.

How are a ▢ and a ▭ alike?

_______________________________________________

How are a ▢ and a ▭ different?

_______________________________________________

TEST YOUR SKILLS

Fun with Bears

Write **>** or **<** to show **greater than** or **less than**.

4 ◯ 7 6 ◯ 5

Fill in the circle for the answer.

| | | | |
|---|---|---|---|
| 4 + 4 = | 6 ◯ | 7 ◯ | 8 ◯ |
| 6 + 2 = | 6 ◯ | 7 ◯ | 8 ◯ |
| 8 – 3 = | 3 ◯ | 4 ◯ | 5 ◯ |
| 7 – 4 = | 3 ◯ | 4 ◯ | 5 ◯ |

Count the sides and corners.

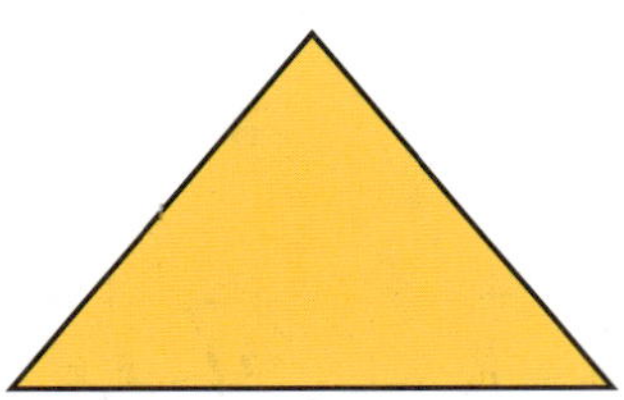

_____ sides

_____ corners

**Skill:**
Add and subtract within 10

Add.

$$\begin{array}{r} 4 \\ +\ 3 \\ \hline \square \end{array}$$

$$\begin{array}{r} 5 \\ +\ 4 \\ \hline \square \end{array}$$

$$\begin{array}{r} 8 \\ +\ 0 \\ \hline \square \end{array}$$

$$\begin{array}{r} 3 \\ +\ 6 \\ \hline \square \end{array}$$

Subtract.

$$\begin{array}{r} 7 \\ -\ 7 \\ \hline \square \end{array}$$

$$\begin{array}{r} 9 \\ -\ 2 \\ \hline \square \end{array}$$

$$\begin{array}{r} 9 \\ -\ 3 \\ \hline \square \end{array}$$

$$\begin{array}{r} 8 \\ -\ 5 \\ \hline \square \end{array}$$

# Bug Problems

Note: You may need to help your child read the word problems.

**Skills:**
Solve word problems; Add and subtract within 10



Read. Write the problems. Solve them.

8  were marching.
3 stopped.

How many ants were still marching?

_____ ants were still marching.

4  were looking for food. 3 more came.

How many ladybugs were there in all?

There were _____ ladybugs in all.

7  were hopping.
2 more came.

How many crickets were hopping then?

_____ crickets were hopping then.

9  were buzzing.
4 stopped.

How many bees were still buzzing?

_____ bees were still buzzing.

# What's the Time?

**Skill:** Tell time to the hour

This clock has 2 hands.

The shorter hand is the **hour hand**. It points to the hour.

The longer hand is the **minute hand**. It points to 12 when a new hour starts.

Write each time in two ways.

**EXAMPLE**

7 o'clock

7 : 00

_____ o'clock

_____ : _____

_____ o'clock

_____ : _____

_____ o'clock

_____ : _____

_____ o'clock

_____ : _____

_____ o'clock

_____ : _____

_____ o'clock

_____ : _____

Creepy Crawlies

**Skill:**
Tell time to the hour

# Match the Times

Draw lines to match the times on the clocks.

Look at the clock. Write the time.

# Busy Ants

**Skills:**
Add and subtract within 10; Use addition and subtraction strategies (addition-subtraction relationship)

Write two addition problems and two subtraction problems.

6 3 9 

6 + 3 = 9

3 + 6 = 9

9 − 3 = 6

9 − 6 = 3

7 2 9 

____ − ____ = ____

____ − ____ = ____

____ + ____ = ____

____ + ____ = ____

7 3 10 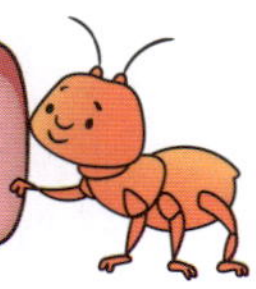

____ + ____ = ____

____ + ____ = ____

____ − ____ = ____

____ − ____ = ____

8 2 10 

____ − ____ = ____

____ − ____ = ____

____ + ____ = ____

____ + ____ = ____

Mark ☒ the one that does **not** belong in the family of facts.

1 + 7 = 8 ☐   7 + 1 = 8 ☐   8 − 1 = 7 ☐   7 − 1 = 6 ☐

Write the missing fact from this family.

____ − ____ = ____

Creepy Crawlies

# What's Missing?

**Skill:**
Add and subtract within 10

Creepy Crawlies

Write the numbers.

2 + 8 = ____

7 + ____ = 7

1 + ____ = 9

4 + ____ = 8

8 − ____ = 0

9 − ____ = 5

6 − ____ = 4

9 − 6 = ____

4 + 6 = ____

**Skill:** Add within 10

Draw circles to make 10. Then write an addition sentence.

**EXAMPLE**

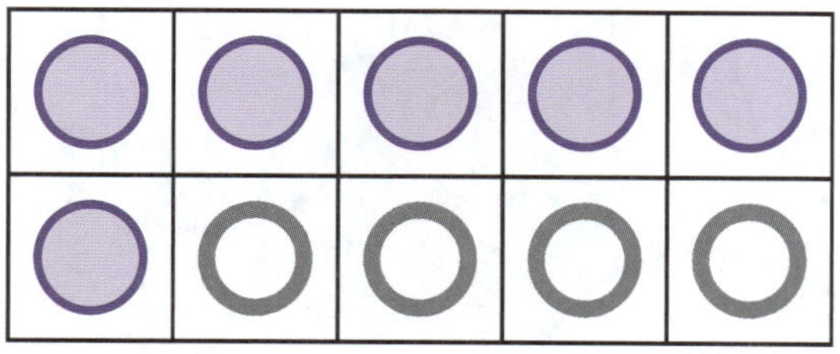

6 + 4 = 10

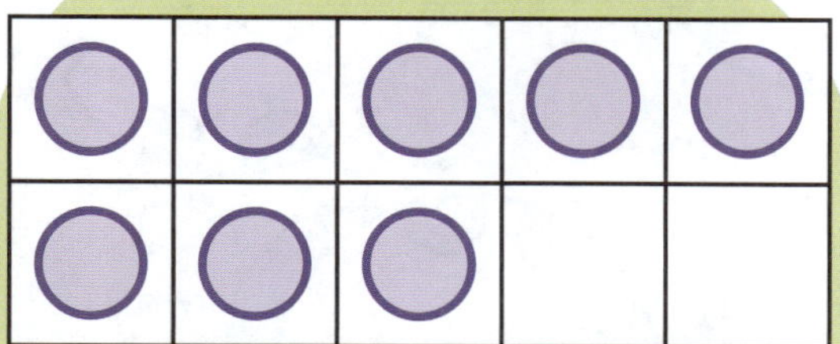

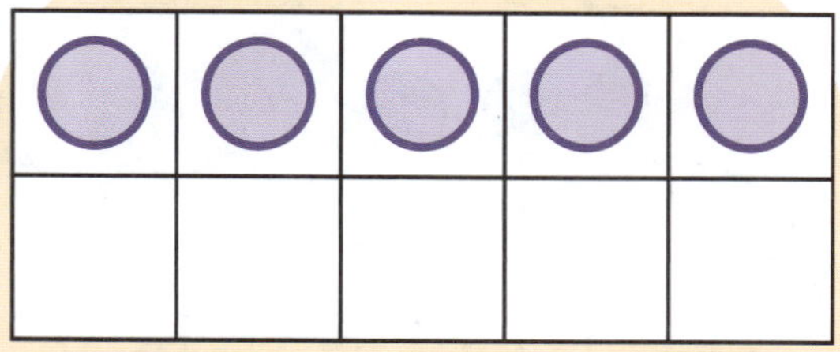

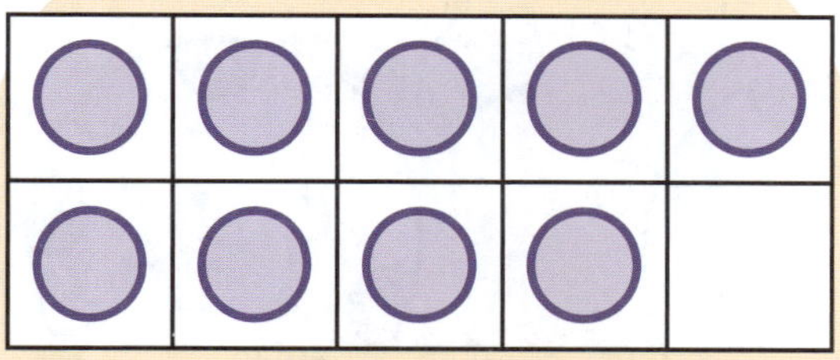

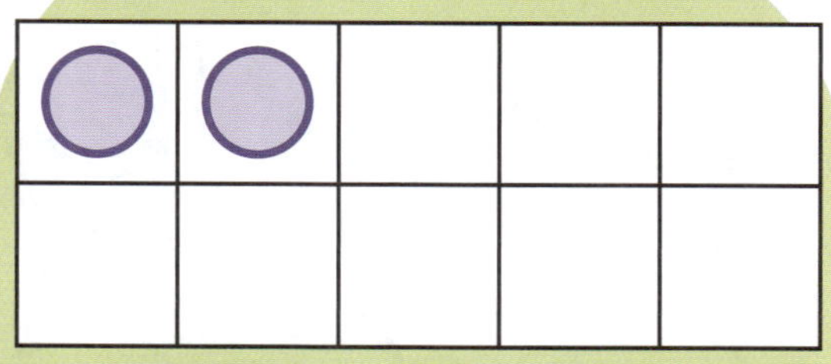

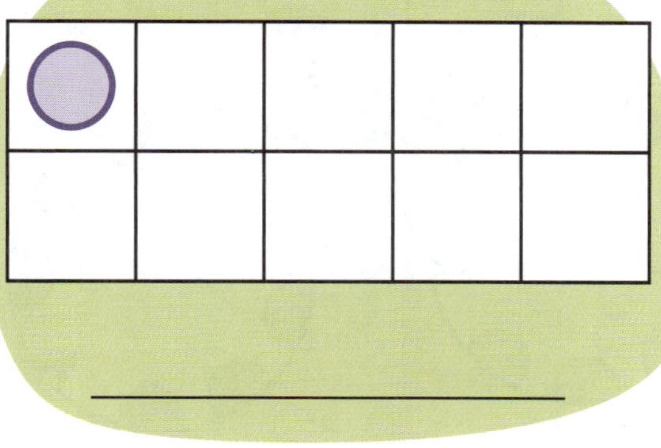

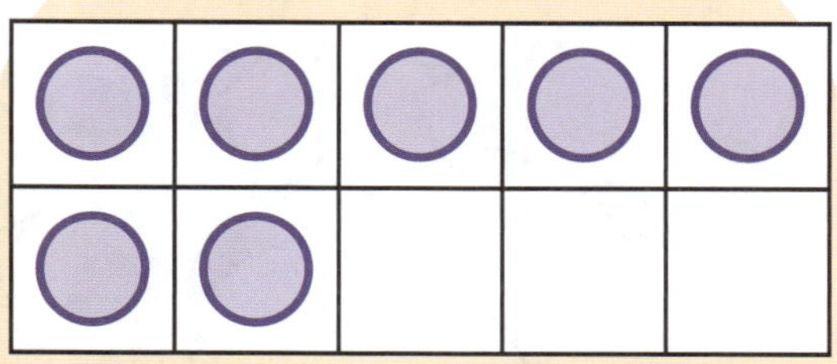

# Ladybugs Are Everywhere!

**Skill:**
Add and subtract within 10

Creepy Crawlies

Add or subtract. Color the ladybugs that = 6.

Add or subtract. Color the ladybugs that = 7.

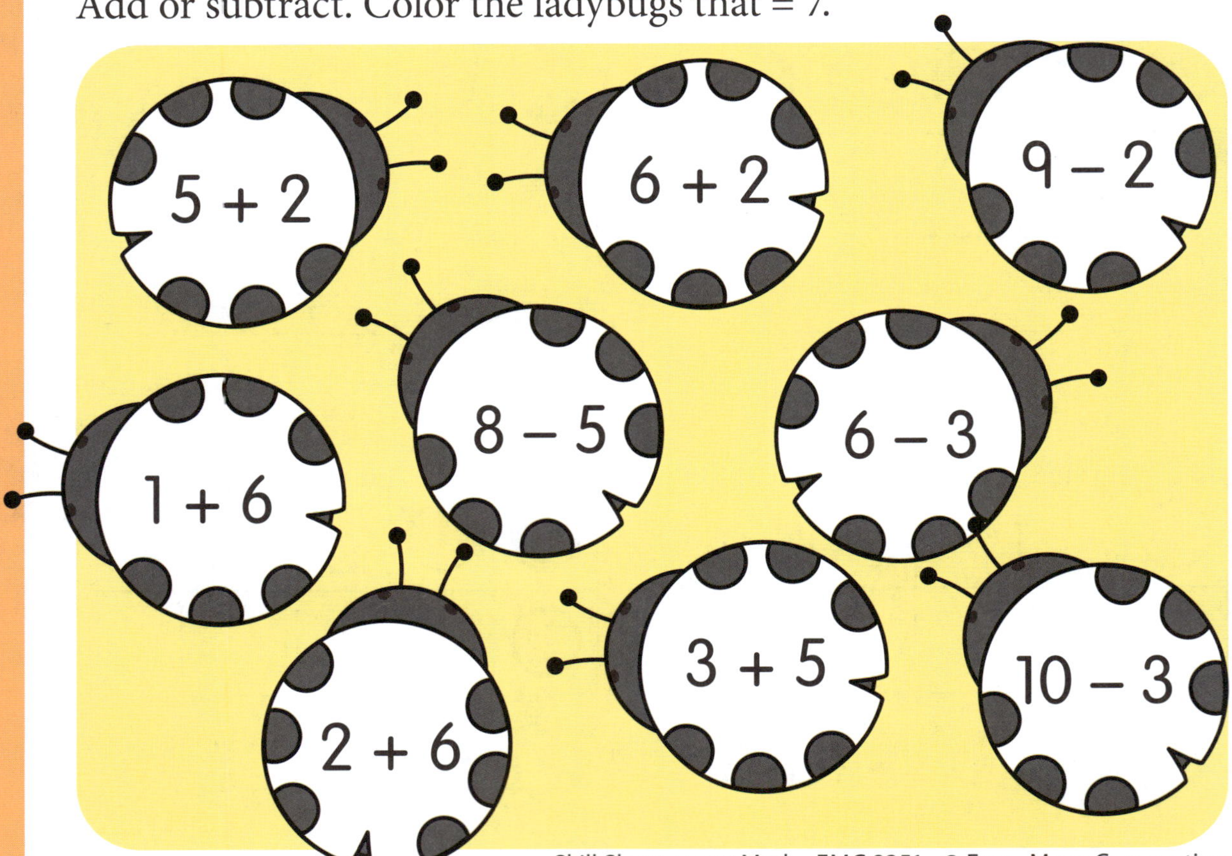

# Bug Stories

**Skills:**
Solve word problems; Add and subtract within 10

Read. Write the problems. Solve them.

9  were crawling. 3 stopped to take a nap.

How many snails were still crawling?

_____ snails were still crawling.

5  were flying. 3 more dragonflies came.

How many dragonflies were flying then?

_____ dragonflies were flying then.

6  were eating grass. All 6 hopped away.

How many grasshoppers were still eating grass?

_____ grasshoppers were still eating grass.

6  were sipping nectar. 4 more butterflies came.

How many butterflies were sipping nectar then?

_____ butterflies were sipping nectar then.

# Garden Friends

**Skills:**
Represent data on a graph; Read a graph

Look at the grass. Count how many.
Color the graph to show how many.

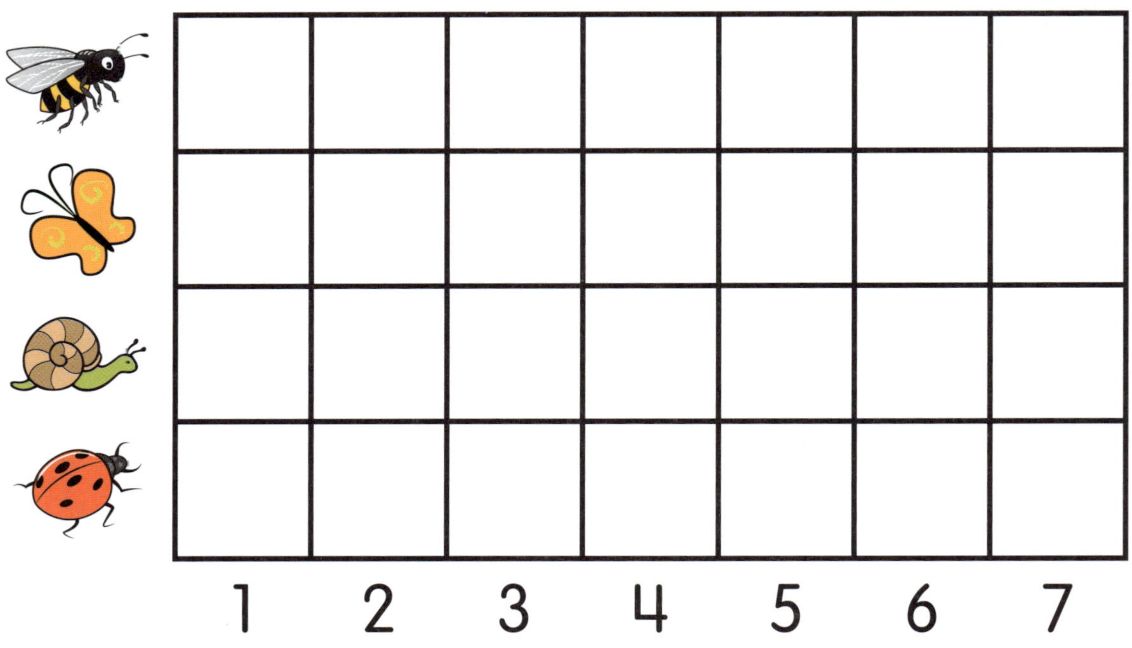


There are the most

There are the least

Which 2 have the same number?

Creepy Crawlies

**Skill:**
Identify and extend patterns

Circle the shape that comes next in each pattern.
Then label the pattern.

**EXAMPLE**

A A B A A B A

# Hungry Caterpillars

**Skill:**
Add and subtract within 10

Creepy Crawlies

Find the answers. Draw a line from each caterpillar to the flower with the correct answer.

Draw a picture to show each number sentence. Write the answer.

5 + 5 = ____

9 – 7 = ____

3 + 6 = ____

Add or subtract.

$3 + 5 =$ ____ $6 + 2 =$ ____ $9 - 6 =$ ____

$7 - 4 =$ ____ $3 + 7 =$ ____ $10 - 1 =$ ____

Write the time in two ways.

____ o'clock ____ o'clock ____ o'clock

____:____ ____:____ ____:____

Draw circles to make 10. Then write an addition sentence.

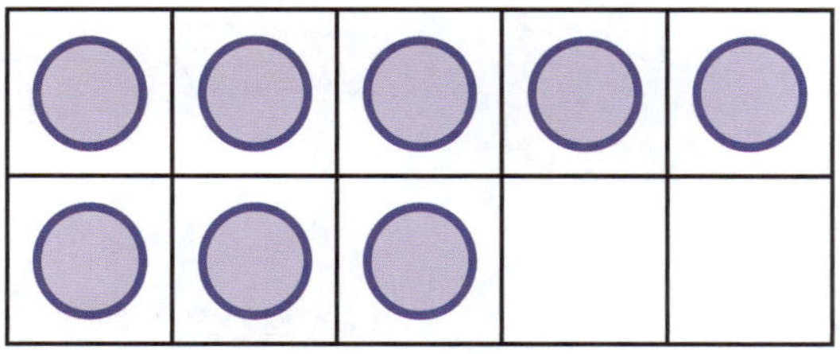

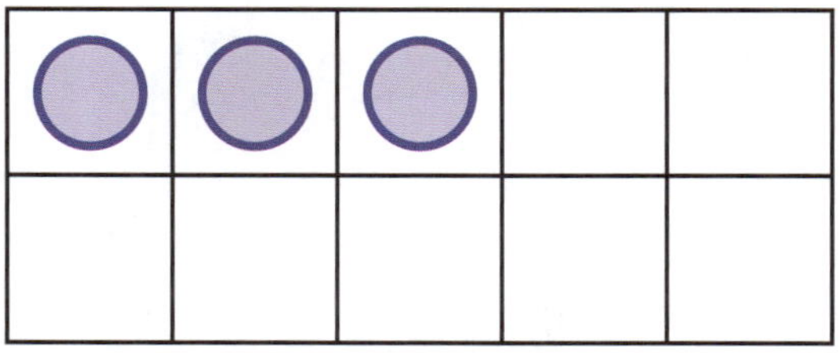

________________ ________________

Finish the pattern. Then label it.

____ ____ ____ ____ ____ ____ ____ ____ ____

# Counting On

**Skill:**
Use addition strategies (counting on)

You can **count on** to add small numbers such as 1, 2, and 3.

**EXAMPLE**

$7 + 2 = ?$

Start with the larger number. It's 7.
Count on 2 more numbers.
You get 7 8 9.

The answer is 9!

6 + 1 = ____

2 + 7 = ____

9 + 2 = ____

1 + 8 = ____

5 + 3 = ____

3 + 7 = ____

8 + 2 = ____

6 + 3 = ____

3 + 9 = ____

8 + 3 = ____

On Safari

**Skill:**
Use subtraction strategies (counting back)

You can **count back** to subtract small numbers such as 1, 2, and 3.

**EXAMPLE**

$8 - 2 = ?$

Start with the first number. It's 8.
Count back 2 more numbers.
You get 8 7 6.

The answer is 6!

$10 - 3 =$ ____

$10 - 2 =$ ____

$8 - 1 =$ ____

$9 - 2 =$ ____

$10 - 1 =$ ____

$9 - 1 =$ ____

$11 - 3 =$ ____

$12 - 3 =$ ____

$11 - 2 =$ ____

$9 - 3 =$ ____

Write two more problems you can solve by counting back.

____ – ____ = ____     ____ – ____ = ____

Note: You may need to help your child read the word problems.

**Skills:**
Add and subtract within 20; Solve word problems



Read. Write the problems. Solve them.

6 zebras were playing. 5 more zebras came to play. How many zebras were playing then?

_6_ + _5_ = _11_

[11] zebras were playing then.

12 elephants were eating. 3 elephants went away. How many elephants were left?

___ − ___ = ___

[ ] elephants were left.

11 lions were sleeping. Then 3 lions woke up. How many lions were still sleeping?

___ − ___ = ___

[ ] lions were still sleeping.

8 ostriches were running. 4 more ostriches joined them. How many ostriches were running then?

___ + ___ = ___

[ ] ostriches were running then.

# Count to 100

**Skill:**
Count within 100

Write the numbers **1** to **100** in order.

| 1 | | | | | | | | | |
|---|---|---|---|---|---|---|---|---|---|
| 11 | | | | | | | | | |
| 21 | | | | | | | | | |
| 31 | | | | | | | | | |
| 41 | | | | | | | | | |
| 51 | | | | | | | | | |
| 61 | | | | | | | | | |
| 71 | | | | | | | | | |
| 81 | | | | | | | | | |
| 91 | | | | | | | | | |

On Safari

# Who Is It?

**Skill:**
Count by 10s

Count by 10s. Then write the numbers.

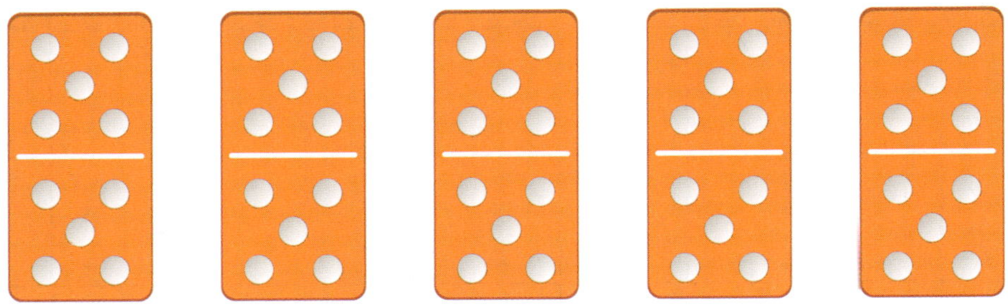

_____ _____ _____ _____ _____

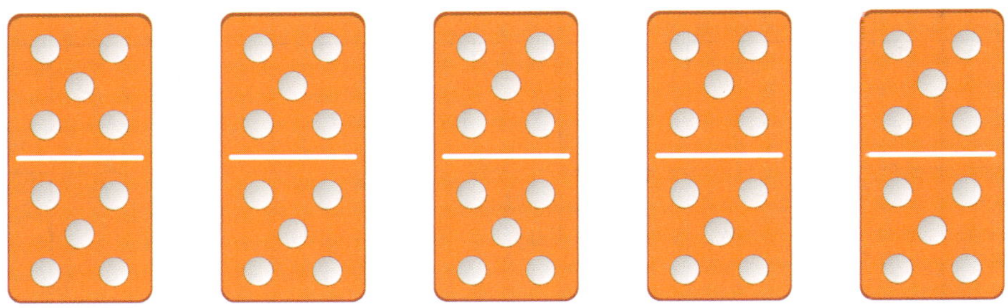

_____ _____ _____ _____ _____

Connect the dots. Start at 10.

**Skill:** Add three numbers

How many?

**EXAMPLE**

$$\begin{array}{r} 3 \\ 1 \\ +\ 4 \\ \hline 8 \end{array}$$

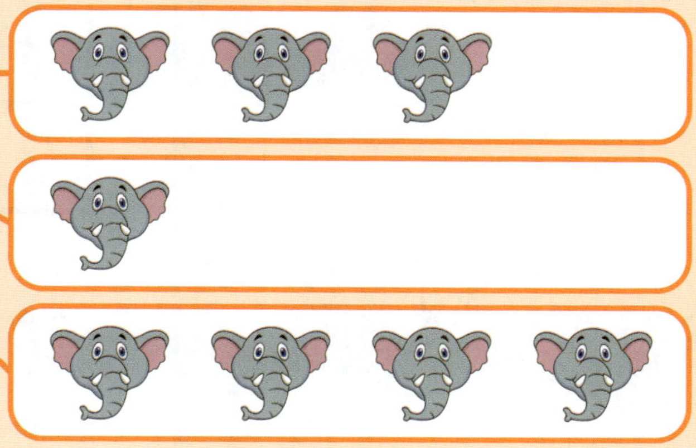

$$\begin{array}{r} 2 \\ 3 \\ +\ 4 \\ \hline \square \end{array} \quad \begin{array}{r} 3 \\ 5 \\ +\ 1 \\ \hline \square \end{array} \quad \begin{array}{r} 6 \\ 1 \\ +\ 2 \\ \hline \square \end{array} \quad \begin{array}{r} 4 \\ 3 \\ +\ 1 \\ \hline \square \end{array} \quad \begin{array}{r} 8 \\ 0 \\ +\ 2 \\ \hline \square \end{array}$$

$$\begin{array}{r} 1 \\ 7 \\ +\ 1 \\ \hline \square \end{array} \quad \begin{array}{r} 1 \\ 6 \\ +\ 3 \\ \hline \square \end{array} \quad \begin{array}{r} 2 \\ 5 \\ +\ 2 \\ \hline \square \end{array} \quad \begin{array}{r} 3 \\ 4 \\ +\ 3 \\ \hline \square \end{array} \quad \begin{array}{r} 4 \\ 3 \\ +\ 2 \\ \hline \square \end{array}$$

$$\begin{array}{r} 5 \\ 2 \\ +\ 3 \\ \hline \square \end{array} \quad \begin{array}{r} 6 \\ 2 \\ +\ 1 \\ \hline \square \end{array} \quad \begin{array}{r} 3 \\ 4 \\ +\ 2 \\ \hline \square \end{array} \quad \begin{array}{r} 5 \\ 2 \\ +\ 1 \\ \hline \square \end{array} \quad \begin{array}{r} 7 \\ 0 \\ +\ 2 \\ \hline \square \end{array}$$

# Mystery Boxes

**Skill:**
Add three numbers

Write the missing numbers.

**EXAMPLE**

7 →, ↓

| | | |
|---|---|---|
| 2 | 3 | 2 |
| 3 | 4 | 0 |
| 2 | 0 | 5 |

2 + 3 + 2 = 7
3 + 4 + 0 = 7
2 + 0 + 5 = 7

2 + 3 + 2 = 7
3 + 4 + 0 = 7
2 + 0 + 5 = 7

8 →, ↓

| | | |
|---|---|---|
| | 2 | 3 |
| | 5 | |
| 3 | | |

9 →, ↓

| | | |
|---|---|---|
| | 3 | 4 |
| | | 2 |
| 5 | 1 | |

10 →, ↓

| | | |
|---|---|---|
| | 3 | |
| 4 | | 2 |
| | 3 | 3 |

On Safari

Circle groups of 10 animals.
How many tens and ones are there?

**Skill:**
Compose numbers with tens and ones

**EXAMPLE**

1 ten + 4 ones = 14

_____ ten + _____ ones = _____

_____ ten + _____ ones = _____

_____ ten + _____ ones = _____

_____ tens + _____ ones = _____

# Tens and Ones

**Skill:**
Compose numbers with tens and ones

Each block is one.
Here are **3 ones**.

There are 10 blocks in this set. This is **1 ten**.

How many?

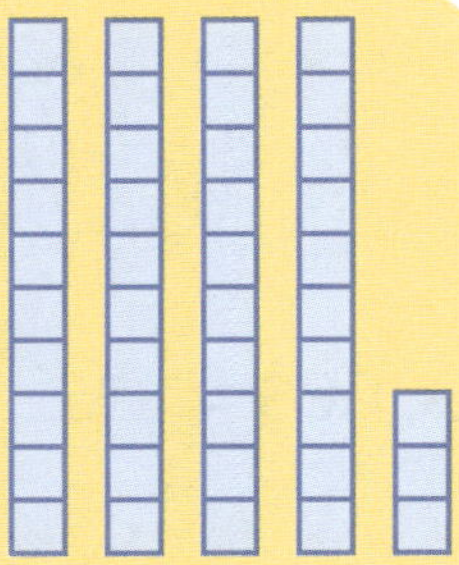
tens ones
4 3
43

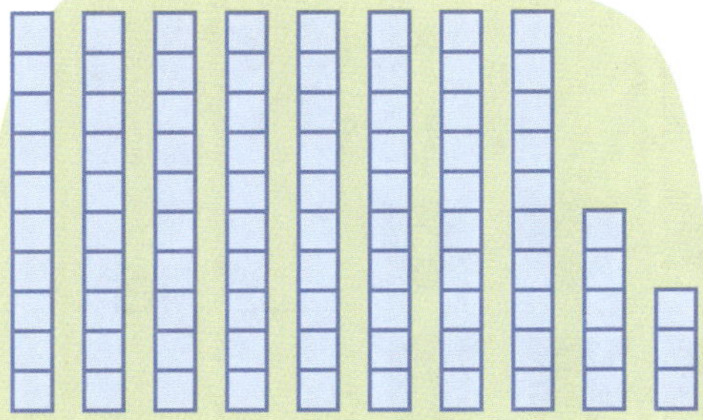
tens ones

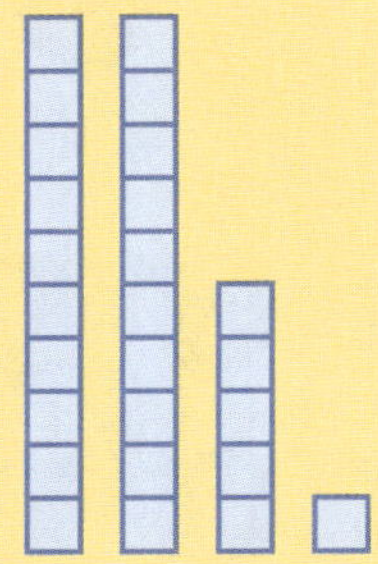
tens ones

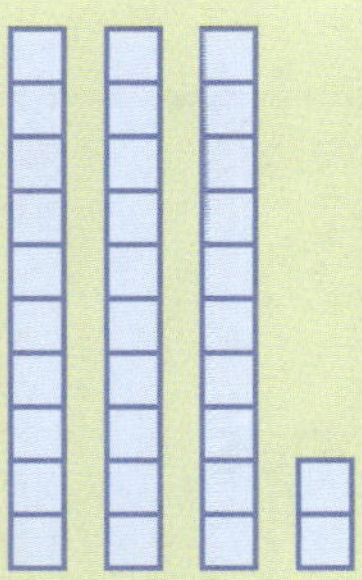
tens ones

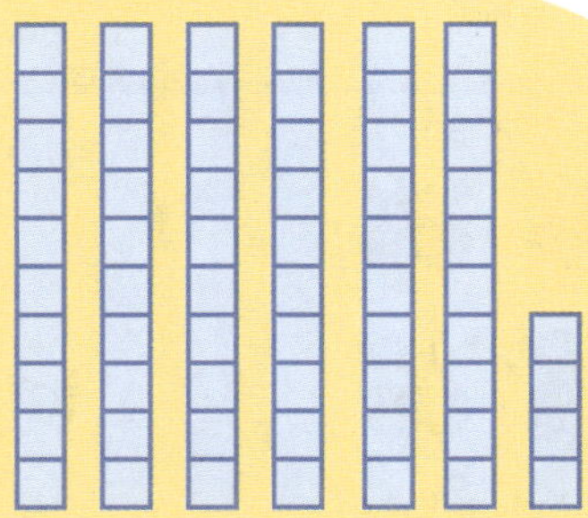
tens ones

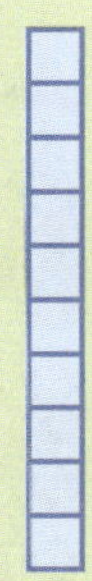
ten ones

On Safari

# Find the Tens

**Skill:** Count by 10s

Count by **tens** to **100**. Then write the numbers.

| 10 | 20 | | | | | | | | |
|---|---|---|---|---|---|---|---|---|---|

Use gray or brown to color the shapes that have the numbers above.

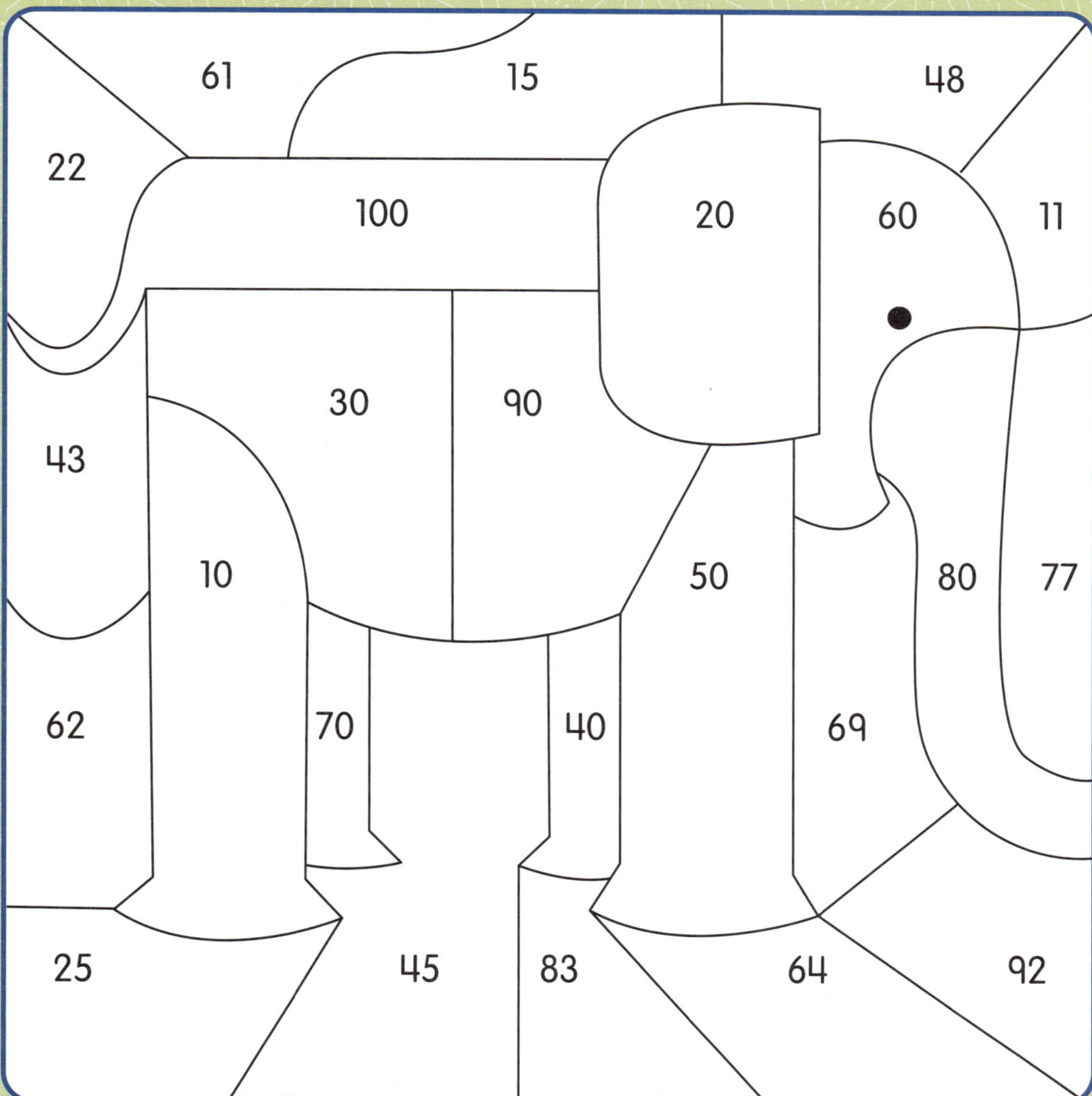

# Animal Toys

**Skill:**
Determine the value of coins

Draw lines to match.

1¢ penny

5¢ nickel

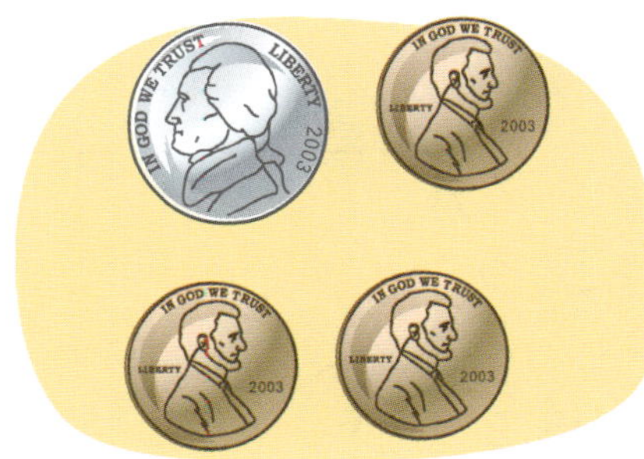

**TEST YOUR SKILLS**

How many?

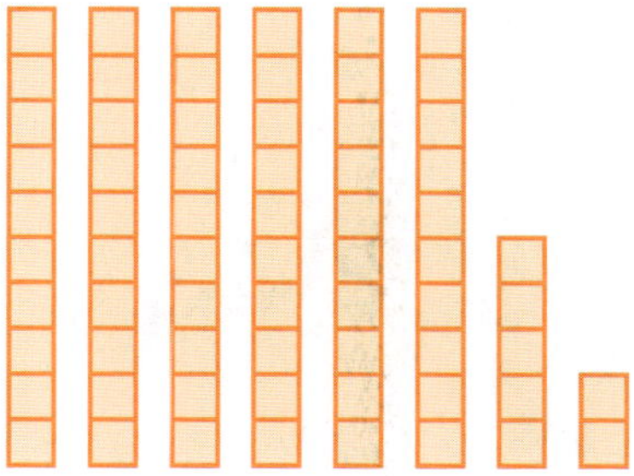

_____ tens + _____ ones = _____

Add or subtract.

8 + 3 = ____    10 – 1 = ____    9 – 2 = ____

2 + 7 = ____    9 + 2 = ____    12 – 3 = ____

Count by 10s.

10, 20, _____, _____, 50, _____, 70, _____, _____, 100

Fill in the circle to show how much.

7¢ ○    12¢ ○    15¢ ○

8¢ ○    9¢ ○    11¢ ○

On Safari!

# Which Tent?

**Skill:**
Add and subtract within 20

Match each problem to its answer.

9 + 2

6 + 4

8 + 3

4 + 8

7 + 4

9 + 3

11 – 4

12 – 5

12 – 4

12 – 3

10 – 0

11 – 2

Let's Go Camping

Fact families are addition facts and subtraction facts that have the same 3 numbers. Make fact families.

3 numbers: **7, 5, 12**

2 addition facts

7 + 5 = 12

5 + 7 = 12

2 subtraction facts

12 – 5 = 7

12 – 7 = 5

**Skills:**

Add and subtract within 20; Use addition and subtraction strategies (addition-subtraction relationship)

**8, 3, 11**

____ + ____ = ____

____ + ____ = ____

____ – ____ = ____

____ – ____ = ____

**9, 4, 13**

____ – ____ = ____

____ – ____ = ____

____ + ____ = ____

____ + ____ = ____

**8, 4, 12**

____ + ____ = ____

____ + ____ = ____

____ – ____ = ____

____ – ____ = ____

**8, 6, 14**

____ – ____ = ____

____ – ____ = ____

____ + ____ = ____

____ + ____ = ____

# Lots of Trees



**Skill:**
Use addition strategies (counting on)

**Count on** to find the sums.

9 + 3 = ?

Start with 9.
Add 3 by counting on.

Solve by counting on. Write the numbers.

8 + 2 = ____

12 + 1 = ____

11 + 3 = ____

9 + 2 = ____

# Busy Campers

**Skills:**
Solve word problems; Add three numbers

Read. Solve the problems.

3 campers went fishing. 5 campers went swimming. 4 campers went hiking. How many campers were there?

_____ campers

Raul is collecting leaves. He finds 4 red leaves, 3 orange leaves, and 7 yellow leaves. How many leaves did he find?

_____ leaves

Kim, Candy, and Maria went fishing. Each girl caught 5 fish. How many fish did they catch in all?

_____ fish

Tony saw birds at camp. He saw 7 jays, 3 hawks, and 4 quails. How many birds did he see?

_____ birds

Write a word problem about this picture. Then write a number sentence for it.

______________________________

______________________________

_____ + _____ + _____ = _____

# Sleepyheads

**Skill:**
Subtract within 20

Use the sleeping bags to help you subtract.

13 – 4 = ____  13 – 6 = ____

13 – 7 = ____  13 – 8 = ____

13 – 9 = ____  13 – 5 = ____

---

14 – 6 = ____  14 – 4 = ____

14 – 7 = ____  14 – 9 = ____

14 – 8 = ____  14 – 5 = ____

Read. Solve the problems.

**Skills:**
Solve word problems;
Add and subtract within 20

There were 13 scouts in Red Troop. 9 scouts went canoeing. The rest of the scouts went fishing. How many scouts went fishing?

_____ scouts went fishing.

Gabe collected 14 leaves. He gave 5 leaves to a friend. How many leaves did Gabe have left?

Gabe had _____ leaves left.

Mary Anne toasted 8 marshmallows. Katie toasted 6 marshmallows. How many marshmallows were toasted in all?

_____ marshmallows were toasted in all.

Blue Troop put up 12 tents. The wind blew down 8 tents. How many tents were still standing?

_____ tents were still standing.

# Camping Gear

**Skill:**
Read a graph

Read the graph. Then answer the questions.

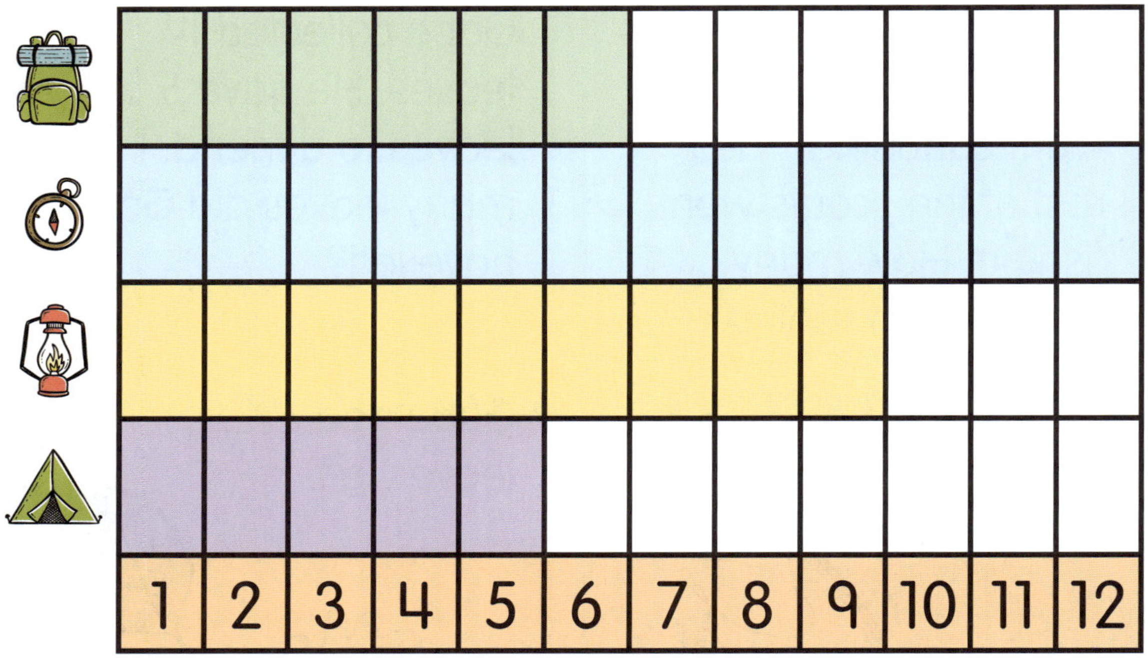


How many are there? ____

How many are there? ____

Are there more or more ?

---

Write the problems. Then answer them.

How many more than are there?

How many and are there in all?

# Through the Woods

**Skills:**
Count within 100; Count by 10s

This is a long path. Count by ones. Write the numbers.

Ten people sleep in each tent. Count by tens to find out how many people are sleeping.

# Before, After, or Between

**Skill:**
Count within 100

Write the missing number.

| after | before | between |
|---|---|---|
| 21 ____ | ____ 47 | 29 ____ 31 |
| 39 ____ | ____ 50 | 43 ____ 45 |
| 45 ____ | ____ 36 | 38 ____ 40 |
| 50 ____ | ____ 64 | 51 ____ 53 |
| 64 ____ | ____ 21 | 67 ____ 69 |
| 77 ____ | ____ 92 | 80 ____ 82 |
| 99 ____ | ____ 63 | 87 ____ 89 |

# How Many Sticks?

**Skill:** Compose numbers with tens and ones

How many tens and ones do you see?

**EXAMPLE**

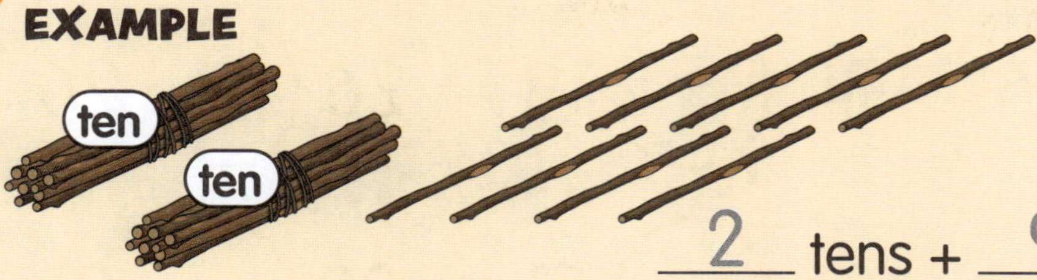


2 tens + 9 ones = 29

_____ tens + _____ ones = 26

_____ tens + _____ ones = 37

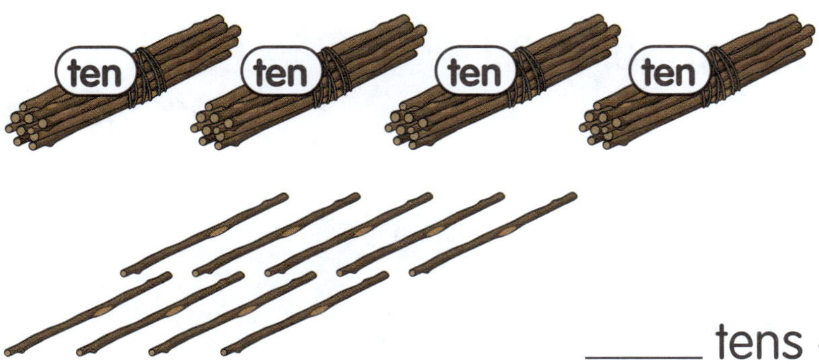


_____ tens + _____ ones = 49

_____ tens + _____ ones = 63

# Comparing Fun

**Skill:** Compare two-digit numbers

Write >, <, or =.

| | | |
|---|---|---|
| 18 ___ 16 | 14 ___ 19 | 26 ___ 26 |
| 43 ___ 40 | 15 ___ 51 | 90 ___ 91 |
| 37 ___ 73 | 21 ___ 12 | 48 ___ 44 |
| 89 ___ 98 | 71 ___ 74 | 77 ___ 77 |

Write a number that is greater than 25. ______

Write a number that is less than 52. ______

Write a number that is equal to 99. ______

# More or Less

**Skills:**
Count within 100; Find 10 more and less than a number

| 1 | 2 | 3 | 4 | 5 | 6 | 7 | 8 | 9 | 10 |
|---|---|---|---|---|---|---|---|---|---|
| 11 | 12 | 13 | 14 | 15 | 16 | 17 | 18 | 19 | 20 |
| 21 | 22 | 23 | 24 | 25 | 26 | 27 | 28 | 29 | 30 |
| 31 | 32 | 33 | 34 | 35 | 36 | 37 | 38 | 39 | 40 |
| 41 | 42 | 43 | 44 | 45 | 46 | 47 | 48 | 49 | 50 |
| 51 | 52 | 53 | 54 | 55 | 56 | 57 | 58 | 59 | 60 |
| 61 | 62 | 63 | 64 | 65 | 66 | 67 | 68 | 69 | 70 |
| 71 | 72 | 73 | 74 | 75 | 76 | 77 | 78 | 79 | 80 |
| 81 | 82 | 83 | 84 | 85 | 86 | 87 | 88 | 89 | 90 |
| 91 | 92 | 93 | 94 | 95 | 96 | 97 | 98 | 99 | 100 |

Write the missing numbers.
Use the number chart to help you.

| | 1 more | 1 less | 10 more | 10 less |
|---|---|---|---|---|
| 12 | ____ | ____ | ____ | ____ |
| 25 | ____ | ____ | ____ | ____ |
| 34 | ____ | ____ | ____ | ____ |
| 49 | ____ | ____ | ____ | ____ |
| 87 | ____ | ____ | ____ | ____ |

TEST YOUR SKILLS

Let's Go Camping

Add or subtract.

5 + 8 = ____ 7 + 7 = ____ 5 + 9 = ____

13 – 4 = ____ 13 – 5 = ____ 15 – 7 = ____

Write the number that comes before, after, or between.

____, 65 36, ____ 79, ____, 81

Write a number sentence to solve the problem.

8 campers went hiking. Then 6 campers joined them. How many campers went hiking?

____ + ____ = ____

Count by 1s.

75 ____ ____ ____ ____ ____ ____ ____ 83

How many tens and ones? How many in all?

____ tens + ____ ones = ____

# A Tasty Crop

**Skill:**
Add and subtract within 20

Add or subtract. Then find the apples with answers that are the same as **3 + 3 + 3**. Color those apples red. Color the other apples yellow.

$7 + 8$

$15 - 7$

$15 - 8$

$8 + 8$

$8 + 7$

$16 - 8$

$16 - 7$

$16 - 9$

$15 - 6$

$9 + 7$

$6 + 9$

$15 - 9$

**Skill:**
Add and subtract within 20



Add or subtract.

6 + 7 = ____
7 + 6 = ____
13 – 7 = ____
13 – 6 = ____

9 + 5 = ____
5 + 9 = ____
14 – 9 = ____
14 – 5 = ____

8 + 6 = ____
6 + 8 = ____
14 – 6 = ____
14 – 8 = ____

8 + 7 = ____
7 + 8 = ____
15 – 7 = ____
15 – 8 = ____

9 + 6 = ____
6 + 9 = ____
15 – 6 = ____
15 – 9 = ____

9 + 7 = ____
7 + 9 = ____
16 – 7 = ____
16 – 9 = ____

Skills:
Solve word problems;
Add and subtract within 20

Read. Write the problems. Solve them.

Dana planted 16 seeds. 7 seeds sprouted. How many seeds did not sprout?

_____ seeds did not sprout.

Jamal picked 8 pears from a tree. Leah picked 7 pears from another tree. How many pears did they pick in all?

They picked _____ pears.

A tree had 8 big plums and 8 little plums. How many plums were on the tree?

There were _____ plums on the tree.

Kimi's tree had 15 apples. Ahmed's tree had 9 apples. How many more apples did Kimi's tree have than Ahmed's tree?

Kimi's tree had _____ more apples.

# Bunches of Grapes

**Skill:**
Compose numbers with tens and ones

Each bunch has 10 grapes.
Add the grapes that are in each set.

**This is 1 ten.**

3 tens + 5 ones = 35

30 + 5 = 35

_____ tens + _____ ones = _____

_____ + _____ = _____

_____ tens + _____ ones = _____

_____ + _____ = _____

---

Add.

60 + 7 = _____ 90 + 2 = _____

70 + 8 = _____ 50 + 5 = _____

# Add the Apples

**Skill:** Compose numbers with tens

Each basket has 10 apples.
Add the apples in each set.

**This is 1 ten.**

__2__ tens + __3__ tens = __5__ tens

__20__ + __30__ = __50__

_____ tens + _____ tens = _____ tens

_____ + _____ = _____

_____ tens + _____ tens = _____ tens

_____ + _____ = _____

Add.

50 + 20 = _____

70 + 10 = _____

30 + 60 = _____

10 + 40 = _____

# Find the Fruits

**Skill:**
Add multiples of 10

Add. Then use the code to color.

red = 60
green = 70
orange = 80
yellow = 90

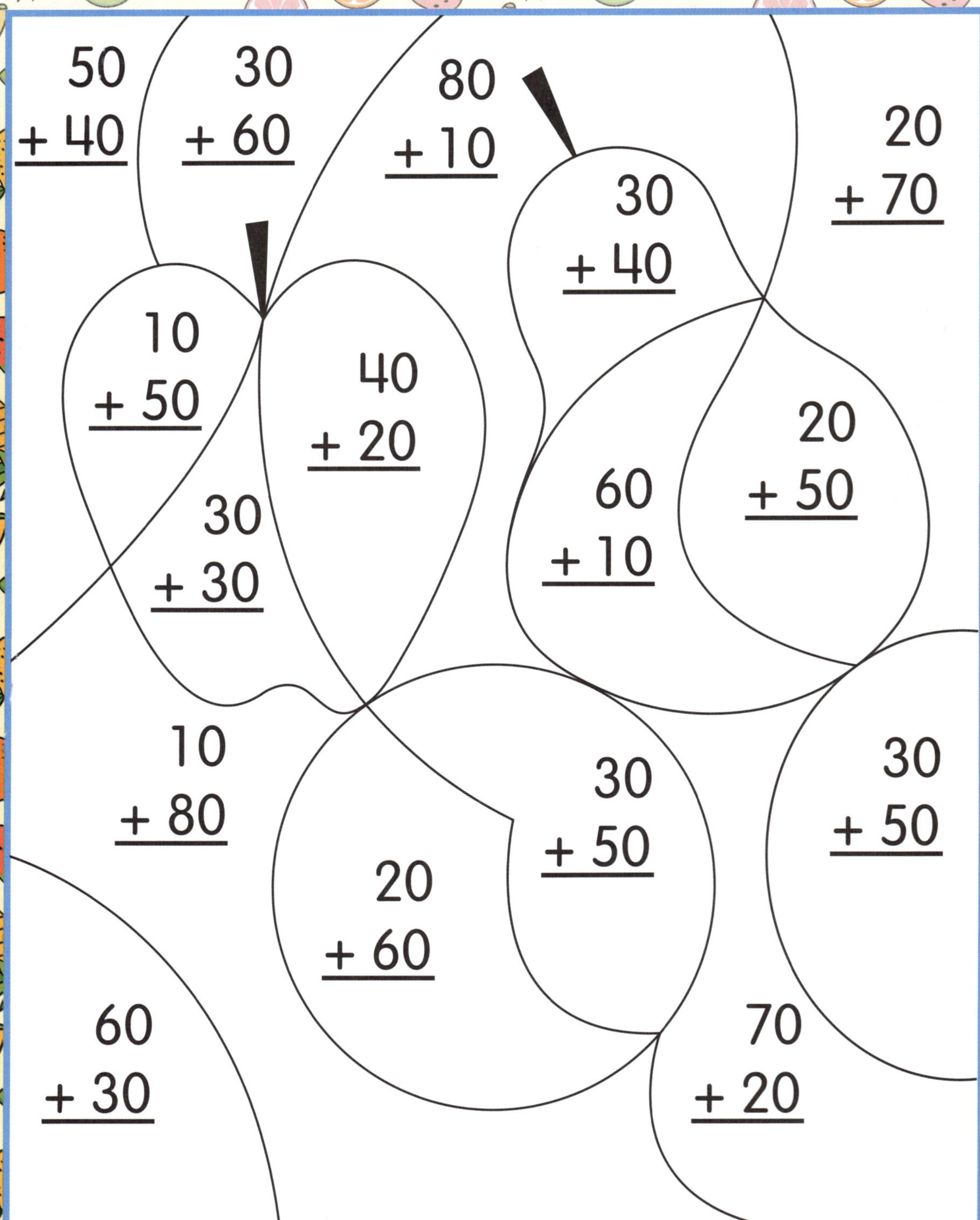

# Farmer Fred's Fruit

**Skills:**
Represent data on a graph; Read a graph

Farmer Fred likes to keep track of the fruit he sells.
Here is what he sold last Saturday.

8 oranges

10 watermelons

7 pineapples

5 pears

Color the graph to show what Farmer Fred sold.

| | | | | | | | | | |
|---|---|---|---|---|---|---|---|---|---|
| | | | | | | | | | |
| | | | | | | | | | |
| | | | | | | | | | |
| | | | | | | | | | |
| 1 | 2 | 3 | 4 | 5 | 6 | 7 | 8 | 9 | 10 |

How many more watermelons were sold than pears? _____ more

How many more oranges were sold than pineapples? _____ more

Circle the fruit that sold the most.

Fruity Fun

# Basket of Shapes

**Skill:** Identify three-dimensional shapes

Follow the directions to color the shapes. Then count them and write the numbers.

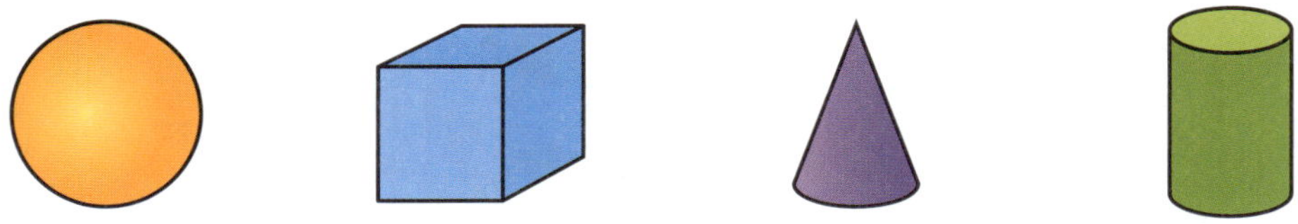

**sphere** **cube** **cone** **cylinder**

Color the spheres yellow. How many do you see? _____

Color the cubes blue. How many do you see? _____

Color the cones purple. How many do you see? _____

Color the cylinders green. How many do you see? _____

**Skill:**
Identify attributes of shapes

Color the fruit that each child likes.

Carla likes fruits that can roll.

Ethan likes fruits that can NOT roll.

Amira likes fruits that can be stacked.

Jin likes fruits that can NOT be stacked.

# A Yummy Treat

**Skill:**
Count by 5s

Count by 5s.

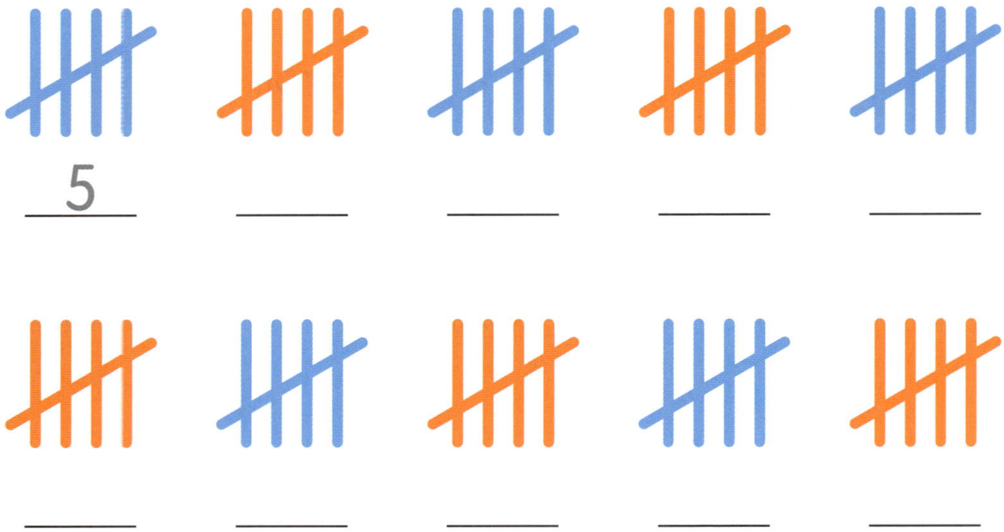


Connect the dots.

Count by 5s to get to the fruit trees.
Fill in the missing numbers.

TEST YOUR SKILLS

Fruity Fun

Add or subtract.

7 + 8 = ____ 16 – 8 = ____ 15 – 6 = ____

9 + 7 = ____ 15 – 7 = ____ 16 – 9 = ____

Count by 5s.

____ ____ ____ ____ ____ ____ ____ ____ ____ ____

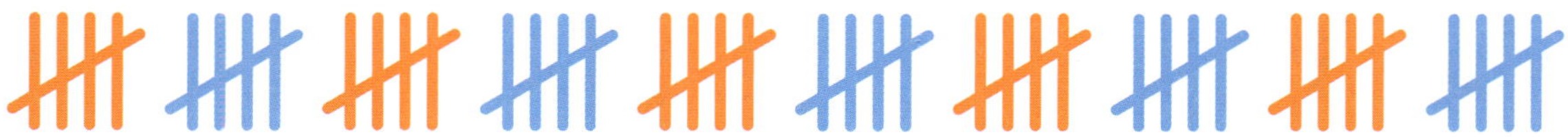

____ ____ ____ ____ ____ ____ ____ ____ ____ ____

Add.

____ tens + ____ tens = ____ tens

____ + ____ = ____

20 + 8 = ____ 70 + 5 = ____

60 + 9 = ____ 30 + 40 = ____

10 + 50 = ____ 50 + 40 = ____

**Skill:**
Add within 20

Add. Color the igloos with a sum of 17 yellow.
Color the igloos with a sum of 18 purple.

8 + 7 = ____

8 + 9 = ____

9 + 6 = ____

8 + 8 = ____

9 + 7 = ____

9 + 8 = ____

9 + 9 = ____

8 + 6 = ____

# Walrus Numbers

**Skills:**

Use addition and subtraction strategies (addition-subtraction relationship); Add and subtract within 20

Use each set of numbers to make two addition problems and two subtraction problems.

**8 6 14**

____ + ____ = ____

____ + ____ = ____

____ − ____ = ____

____ − ____ = ____

**7 8 15**

____ + ____ = ____

____ + ____ = ____

____ − ____ = ____

____ − ____ = ____

**9 7 16**

____ + ____ = ____

____ + ____ = ____

____ − ____ = ____

____ − ____ = ____

**8 9 17**

____ + ____ = ____

____ + ____ = ____

____ − ____ = ____

____ − ____ = ____

**Skills:**
Solve word problems;
Add and subtract within 20

Read. Write the problems. Solve them.

9 penguins were swimming in the sea. 8 more penguins jumped in. How many penguins were swimming in the sea then?

☐ + ☐ = ☐

There were _____ penguins swimming in the sea then.

16 walruses were lying on the ice. 9 walruses slid back into the sea. How many walruses were still on the ice?

☐ – ☐ = ☐

There were _____ walruses still on the ice.

Polar Bear saw 6 seals in the morning and 9 seals in the afternoon. How many seals did Polar Bear see that day?

☐ + ☐ = ☐

Polar Bear saw _____ seals that day.

18 seals were playing in the water. 9 seals swam away. How many seals were still playing?

☐ – ☐ = ☐

There were _____ seals still playing.

# Seeing Double

**Skill:**
Use addition and subtraction strategies (doubles)

Add.

$\begin{array}{r} 2 \\ +\ 2 \\ \hline \end{array}$ $\begin{array}{r} 3 \\ +\ 3 \\ \hline \end{array}$ $\begin{array}{r} 1 \\ +\ 1 \\ \hline \end{array}$ $\begin{array}{r} 5 \\ +\ 5 \\ \hline \end{array}$ $\begin{array}{r} 4 \\ +\ 4 \\ \hline \end{array}$

$\begin{array}{r} 6 \\ +\ 6 \\ \hline \end{array}$ $\begin{array}{r} 8 \\ +\ 8 \\ \hline \end{array}$ $\begin{array}{r} 7 \\ +\ 7 \\ \hline \end{array}$ $\begin{array}{r} 9 \\ +\ 9 \\ \hline \end{array}$

$\begin{array}{r} 10 \\ +\ 10 \\ \hline \end{array}$

Use the doubles addition facts to help you subtract.

$\begin{array}{r} 12 \\ -\ 6 \\ \hline \end{array}$ $\begin{array}{r} 16 \\ -\ 8 \\ \hline \end{array}$ $\begin{array}{r} 18 \\ -\ 9 \\ \hline \end{array}$ $\begin{array}{r} 14 \\ -\ 7 \\ \hline \end{array}$

# Catch of the Day

**Skills:**
Add two-digit numbers; Add multiples of 10

Add.

**EXAMPLE**

$$\begin{array}{r} 24 \\ +\,30 \\ \hline 54 \end{array}$$

$$\begin{array}{r} 15 \\ +\,10 \\ \hline \end{array} \qquad \begin{array}{r} 24 \\ +\,20 \\ \hline \end{array} \qquad \begin{array}{r} 18 \\ +\,60 \\ \hline \end{array}$$

$$\begin{array}{r} 27 \\ +\,20 \\ \hline \end{array} \qquad \begin{array}{r} 39 \\ +\,30 \\ \hline \end{array}$$

$$\begin{array}{r} 27 \\ +\,40 \\ \hline \end{array} \qquad \begin{array}{r} 21 \\ +\,50 \\ \hline \end{array} \qquad \begin{array}{r} 16 \\ +\,70 \\ \hline \end{array}$$

$$\begin{array}{r} 83 \\ +\,10 \\ \hline \end{array} \qquad \begin{array}{r} 52 \\ +\,30 \\ \hline \end{array} \qquad \begin{array}{r} 35 \\ +\,40 \\ \hline \end{array}$$

# Snowball Subtraction

**Skill:**
Subtract multiples of 10

There are 10 snowballs in each pile.
Cross out the piles to help you subtract.

**EXAMPLE**

5 tens – 2 tens = __3__ tens

__50__ – __20__ = __30__

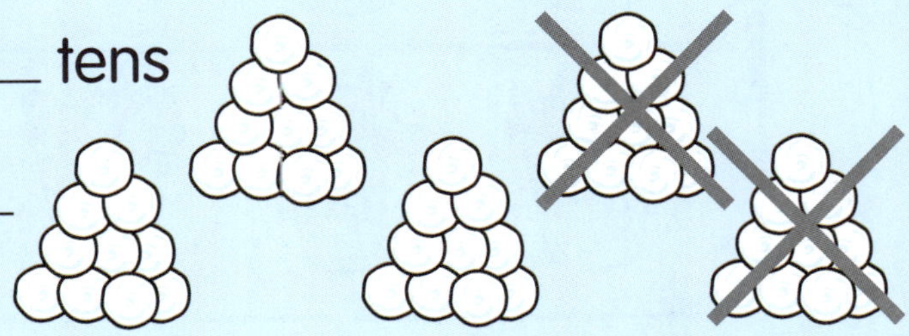

3 tens – 1 ten = _____ tens

_____ – _____ = _____

4 tens – 3 tens = _____ ten

_____ – _____ = _____

5 tens – 3 tens = _____ tens

_____ – _____ = _____

Subtract.

$$\begin{array}{r} 60 \\ -\ 50 \\ \hline \end{array} \qquad \begin{array}{r} 80 \\ -\ 30 \\ \hline \end{array} \qquad \begin{array}{r} 70 \\ -\ 10 \\ \hline \end{array} \qquad \begin{array}{r} 90 \\ -\ 40 \\ \hline \end{array}$$

Add or subtract.

| | | |
|---|---|---|
| $15 + 30$ | $20 + 60$ | $82 - 20$ |
| $60 + 30$ | $90 - 20$ | $70 - 50$ |
| $40 + 40$ | $60 - 30$ | $30 + 40$ |

**Skills:**

Add and subtract two-digit numbers; Add and subtract multiples of 10

**Skill:**
Determine value of coins

# Winter Stickers

Add the coins. Write the price on the tag.

penny
1¢

nickel
5¢

dime
10¢

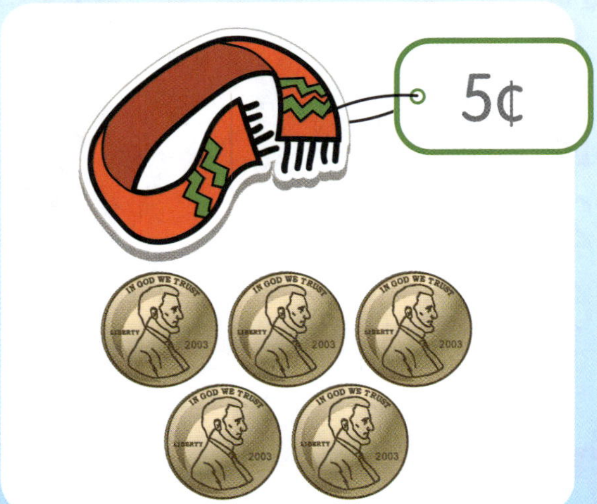

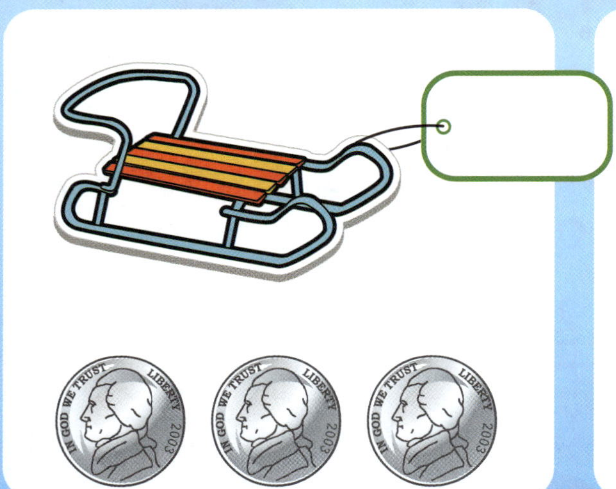

**Skill:**
Tell time to the half hour

Write the time.

____ : ____

____ : ____

____ : ____

____ : ____

____ : ____

____ : ____

____ : ____

____ : ____

____ : ____

# How Many Fish?

**Skill:**
Count by 2s, 5s, and 10s

Circle pairs of fish. Count by 2s. Write how many.

Count by 5s.

5, _____, _____, 20, _____, 30, _____, _____, _____, 50

Count by 10s.

10, _____, _____, 40, _____, _____, _____, 80, _____, _____

**Skill:**
Count by 2s

Count the mittens by 2s.

2    4    ____    ____    ____

12    ____    ____    ____    ____

Count by 2s to slide down the hill.

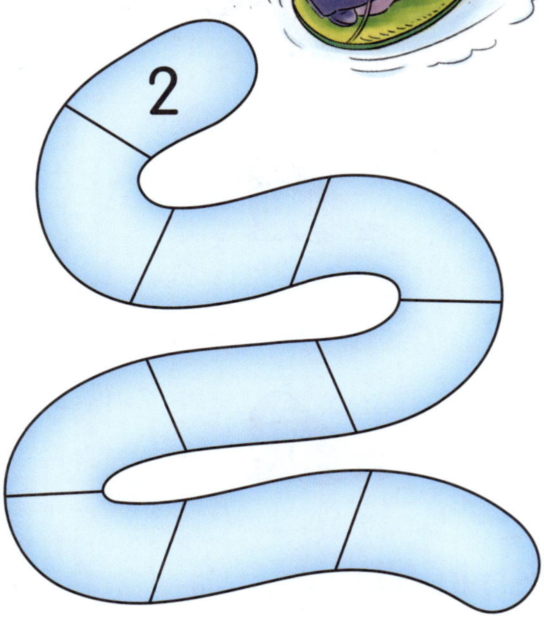


Connect the dots. Color.

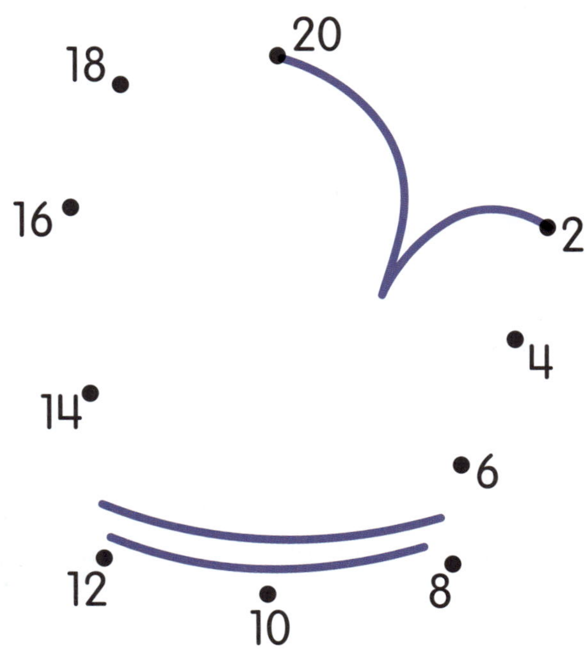

# Fish-Eating Contest

**Skill:**
Read a graph

Use the graph to find out how many fish the animals ate. Then answer the questions.

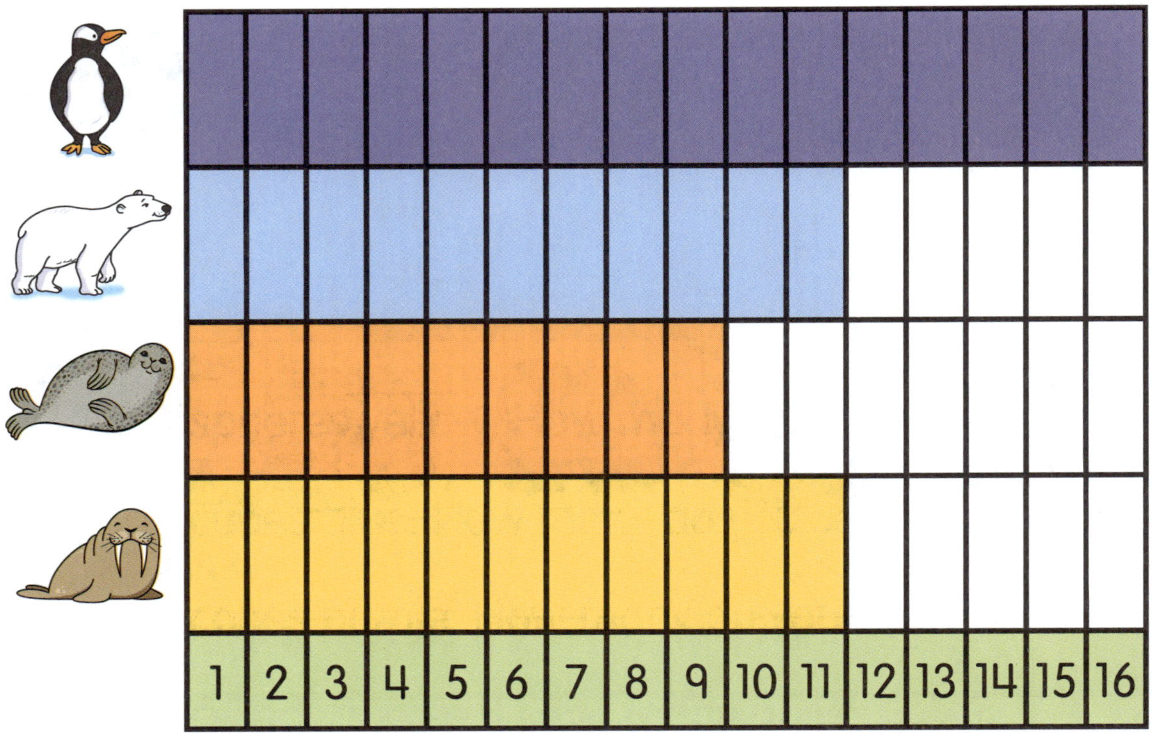


How many fish did each animal eat?

Which animal ate the most fish?

Which animal ate the fewest fish?

Polar Bear and Seal ate _____ fish in all.

Penguin ate _____ more fish than Walrus.

Chilly Capers

Add or subtract.

8 + 9 = ____ 9 + 9 = ____ 9 + 8 = ____

17 – 9 = ____ 17 – 8 = ____ 18 – 9 = ____

Count by 2s.

____, ____, 6, ____, 10, 12, 14, ____, ____, 20

There were 9 gray seals and 8 brown seals.
How many seals were there?

____ + ____ = ____ There were ____ seals.

Add or subtract.

| | | | |
|---|---|---|---|
| 49 | 27 | 80 | 70 |
| + 50 | + 30 | – 60 | – 20 |

Write the time.

____ : ____

____ : ____

# Colorful Balloons

**Skill:**
Use addition strategies (make 10)

First add two numbers to make 10.
Then add the last number.

| Numbers | Make 10 | Add the last number |
|---|---|---|
| 7, 3, + 4 | 10 | + 4 = 14 |
| 1, 9, + 2 | ☐ | + 2 = ___ |
| 8, 2, + 3 | ☐ | + 3 = ___ |
| 4, 6, + 7 | ☐ | + 7 = ___ |
| 3, 7, + 5 | ☐ | + 5 = ___ |
| 9, 1, + 8 | ☐ | + 8 = ___ |
| 5, 5, + 6 | ☐ | + 6 = ___ |
| 2, 8, + 9 | ☐ | + 9 = ___ |
| 6, 4, + 5 | ☐ | + 5 = ___ |

**Skill:** Use addition strategies (make 10)



Circle the balls needed to make a group of 10.
Then finish adding the rest.

**7 + 5 = ?**

7 + __3__ = 10 10 + __2__ = __12__

**9 + 4 = ?**

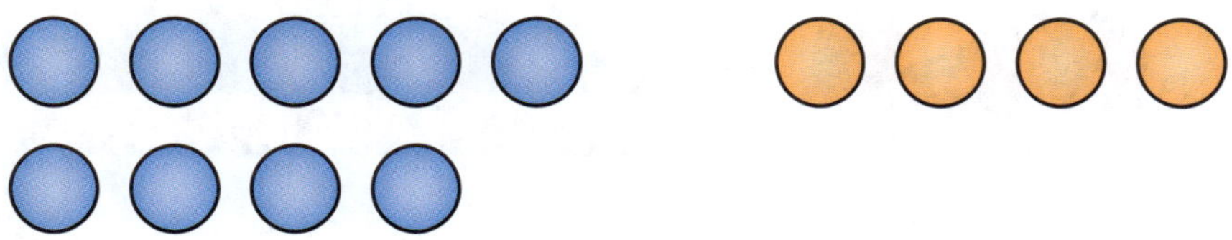

9 + ____ = 10 10 + ____ = ____

**6 + 7 = ?**

6 + ____ = 10 10 + ____ = ____

**8 + 6 = ?**

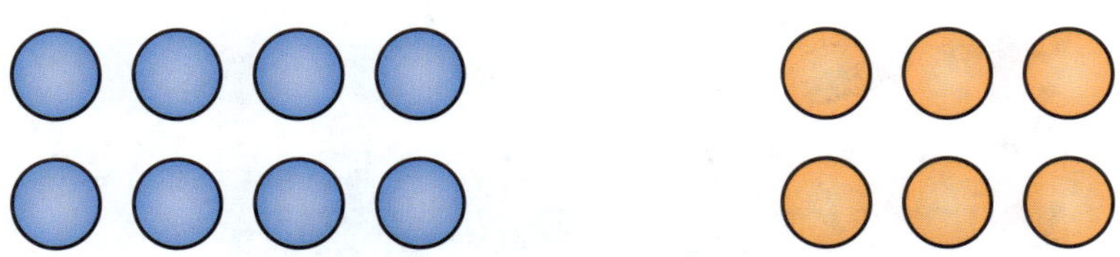

8 + ____ = 10 10 + ____ = ____

# Number Carts

**Skill:**
Add within 20

Add.

$6 + \_\_\_\_ = 13$

$8 + \_\_\_\_ = 14$

$\_\_\_\_ + 9 = 18$

$\_\_\_\_ + 7 = 12$

$9 + \_\_\_\_ = 17$

$5 + \_\_\_\_ = 14$

$\_\_\_\_ + 8 = 16$

$\_\_\_\_ + 9 = 15$

Fill your own cart.

$\_\_\_\_ + \_\_\_\_ = \_\_\_\_$

$\_\_\_\_ + \_\_\_\_ = \_\_\_\_$

# A Roller Coaster Ride

**Skills:**
Add two-digit numbers; Add multiples of 10

Add.

| | | | | |
|---|---|---|---|---|
| 46 + 30 | 20 + 30 | 70 + 8 | 51 + 40 | 73 + 20 |
| 36 + 60 | 50 + 30 | 80 + 9 | 42 + 40 | 15 + 40 |
| 17 + 60 | 12 + 80 | 29 + 20 | 10 + 50 | 20 + 50 |

# Tasty Treats

Note: You may need to help your child read the word problems.

**Skills:**
Solve word problems; Add and subtract two-digit numbers; Add and subtract multiples of 10

At the Fair

Read. Write the problems. Solve them.

Kai sold ice cream cones at the fair. He sold 35 cones before lunch. He sold 40 cones after lunch. How many ice cream cones did he sell at the fair?

Kai sold _____ ice cream cones.

---

Jason bought a bag of peanuts. There were 50 peanuts in the bag. Jason ate 20 peanuts. How many peanuts were left?

There were _____ peanuts left.

---

Anna sold 27 bags of popcorn. Sam sold 30 bags of popcorn. How many bags did they sell together?

They sold _____ bags of popcorn.

---

80 people bought cotton candy yesterday. 60 people bought cotton candy today. How many more people bought cotton candy yesterday than today?

_____ more people bought cotton candy yesterday.

**Skills:**
Subtract two-digit numbers; Subtract multiples of 10

Cross out tens to help you subtract.

**54 – 20**

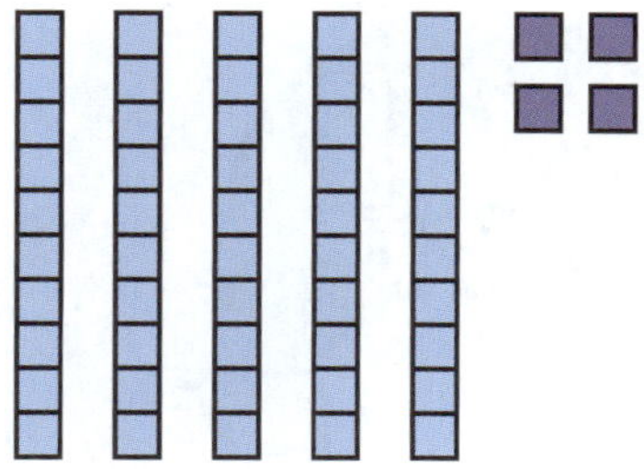

54 – 20 = ____

**38 – 20**

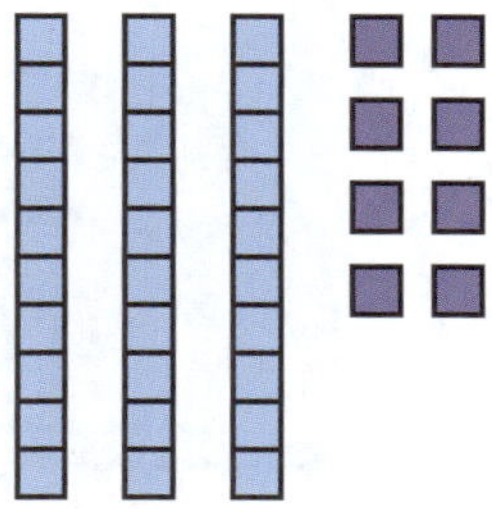

38 – 20 = ____

**42 – 10**

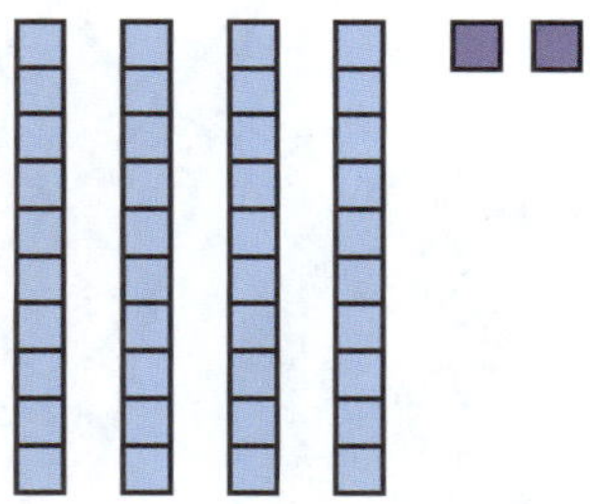

42 – 10 = ____

**57 – 40**

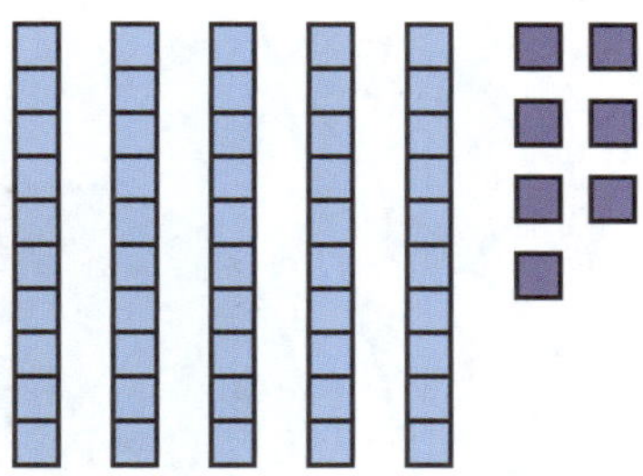

57 – 40 = ____

**69 – 30**

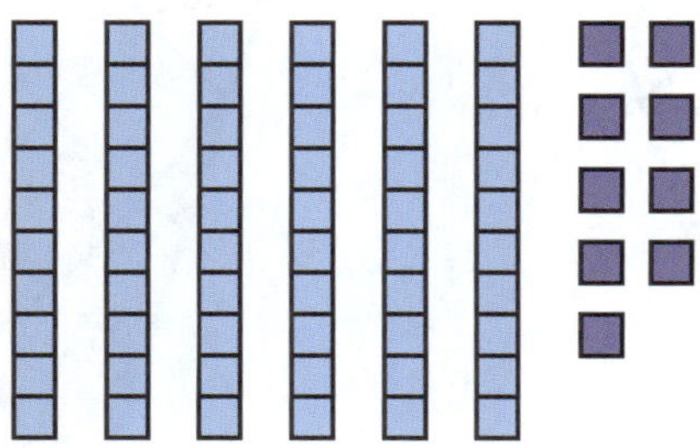

69 – 30 = ____

# Cool Subtraction

**Skills:**

Subtract two-digit numbers; Subtract multiples of 10

Subtract.

$$\begin{array}{r} 65 \\ -\ 40 \\ \hline \end{array}$$

$$\begin{array}{r} 81 \\ -\ 50 \\ \hline \end{array}$$

$$\begin{array}{r} 39 \\ -\ 10 \\ \hline \end{array}$$

$$\begin{array}{r} 75 \\ -\ 30 \\ \hline \end{array}$$

$$\begin{array}{r} 28 \\ -\ 10 \\ \hline \end{array}$$

$$\begin{array}{r} 47 \\ -\ 20 \\ \hline \end{array}$$

$$\begin{array}{r} 96 \\ -\ 70 \\ \hline \end{array}$$

$$\begin{array}{r} 52 \\ -\ 40 \\ \hline \end{array}$$

$$\begin{array}{r} 88 \\ -\ 60 \\ \hline \end{array}$$

$$\begin{array}{r} 73 \\ -\ 20 \\ \hline \end{array}$$

**Skill:** Identify equal shares

How many equal parts are there?

_____ parts _____ parts _____ part

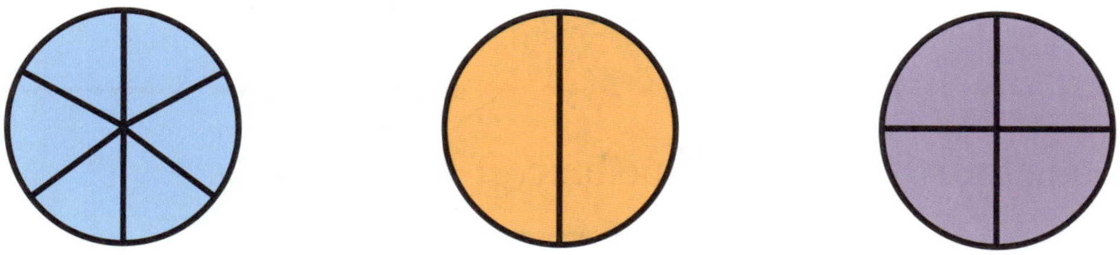

_____ parts _____ parts _____ parts

Which shapes have 2 **equal** parts? Circle them.

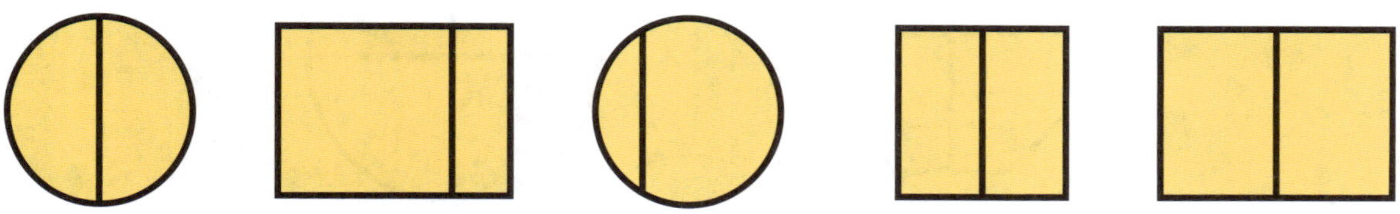

Which shapes have 4 **equal** parts? Circle them.

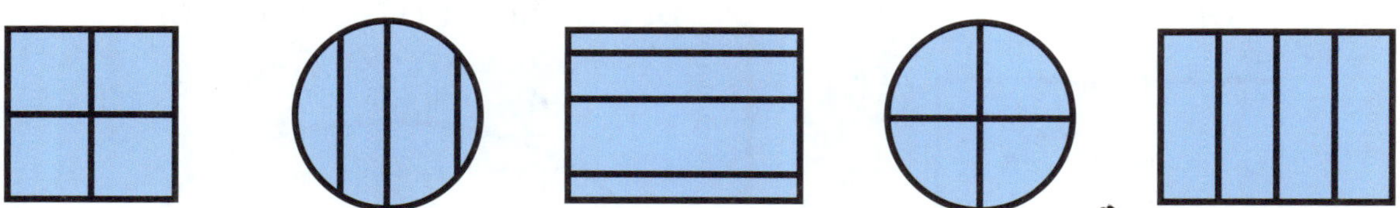

# Fraction Fun

**Skill:**
Identify equal shares

Color one half of each shape green.

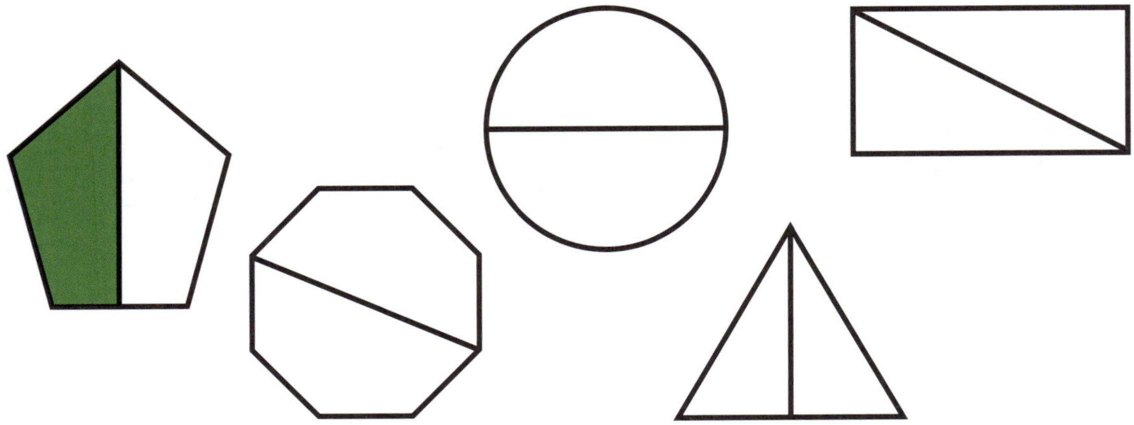

Color one fourth of each shape blue.

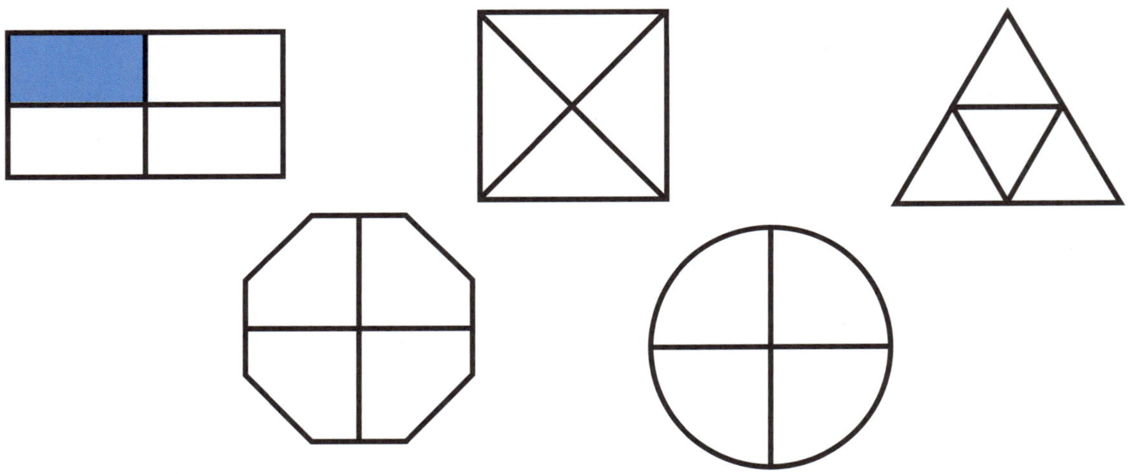

Draw a line to make 2 equal parts. Color one half green.

Draw lines to make 4 equal parts. Color one fourth blue.

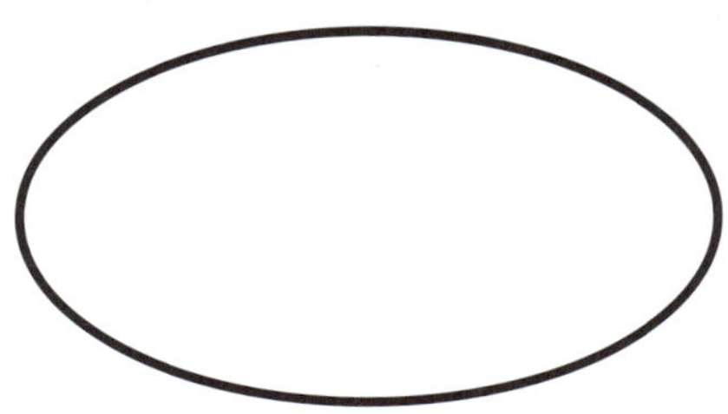

# When Will They Go?

Six families are going to the fair at different times.
Draw lines to match the clocks.

**Skill:**
Tell time to the half hour

Jones family

Eng family

Lee family

Santos family

Sidhu family

Miller family

# The Great Caterpillar Race

**Skill:** Measure length using centimeters

The fair had a Great Caterpillar Race.
How long were the racers?

______ centimeters

______ centimeters

______ centimeters

______ centimeters

Which caterpillar was the longest—
orange, green, blue, or purple? ____________________

TEST YOUR SKILLS

Fill in the missing numbers.

7 + ____ = 13   8 + ____ = 15   6 + ____ = 15

____ + 9 = 17   ____ + 5 = 14   ____ + 8 = 16

Add or subtract.

78 – 30 = ____   63 + 20 = ____

45 + 20 = ____   91 – 50 = ____

Blair sold 56 bags of popcorn on Monday and 40 bags on Tuesday. How many bags of popcorn did Blair sell?

Blair sold ____ bags of popcorn.

Circle the shapes that have one fourth colored.

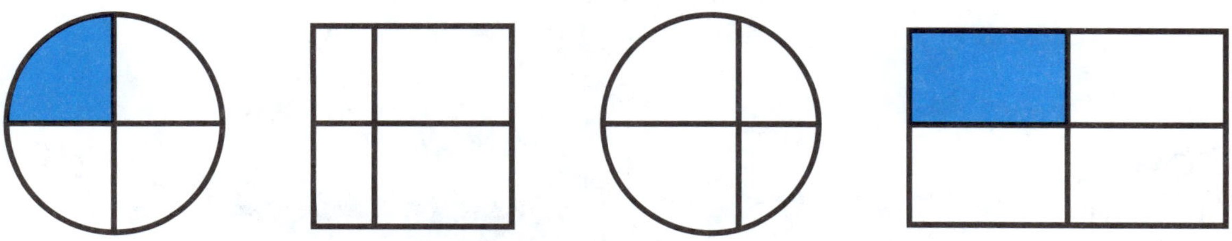

How long?

____ centimeters

At the Fair

# Play Catch

**Skill:**
Add and subtract within 20

Add or subtract. Draw lines to match the balls and gloves.

| Balls | Gloves | Balls |
| --- | --- | --- |
| $9 + 3$ | 11 | $15 - 4$ |
| $3 + 8$ | 12 | $9 + 4$ |
| $17 - 3$ | 13 | $19 - 7$ |
| $19 - 4$ | 14 | $8 + 5$ |
| $8 + 6$ | 15 | $18 - 2$ |
| $8 + 8$ | 16 | $9 + 6$ |

**Skill:** Add three numbers

Use the numbers on the tennis balls to complete each problem.

3  2  6  0  12  10  9  5

| | | | |
|---|---|---|---|
| 4 | 2 | 8 | 6 |
| ☐ | 3 | 1 | 0 |
| + 3 | + 4 | + ☐ | + ☐ |
| 10 | ☐ | 11 | 11 |

| | | | |
|---|---|---|---|
| 1 | ☐ | 2 | 4 |
| 9 | 5 | ☐ | 4 |
| + 0 | + 5 | + 4 | + 4 |
| ☐ | 10 | 12 | ☐ |

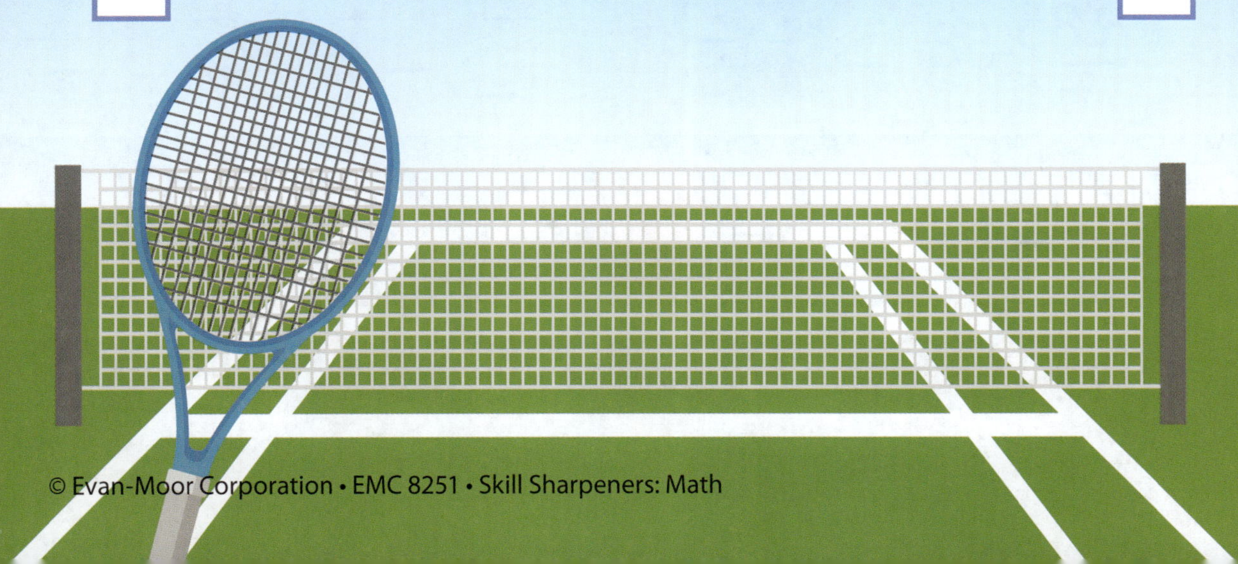

# Let's Bowl



**Skill:**
Sequence two-digit numbers

Write the numbers in order from the least to the greatest.

**EXAMPLE**

15 5 50 — 5 15 50

43 14 34 — ____ ____ ____

76 67 77 — ____ ____ ____

19 99 90 — ____ ____ ____

80 85 58 — ____ ____ ____

# Hockey Practice

**Skill:**
Add two-digit numbers

Add. You can break up numbers to help you.

**EXAMPLE**

```
  31         30 + 1
+ 64   →     60 + 4
             ---------
             90 + 5 = 95
```

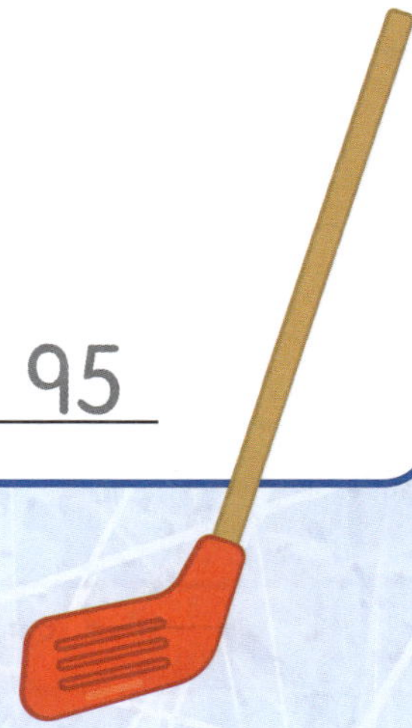

```
  15         ___ + ___
+ 42   →     ___ + ___
             ---------
             ___ + ___ = ___
```

```
  23         ___ + ___
+ 75   →     ___ + ___
             ---------
             ___ + ___ = ___
```

```
  52         ___ + ___
+ 24   →     ___ + ___
             ---------
             ___ + ___ = ___
```

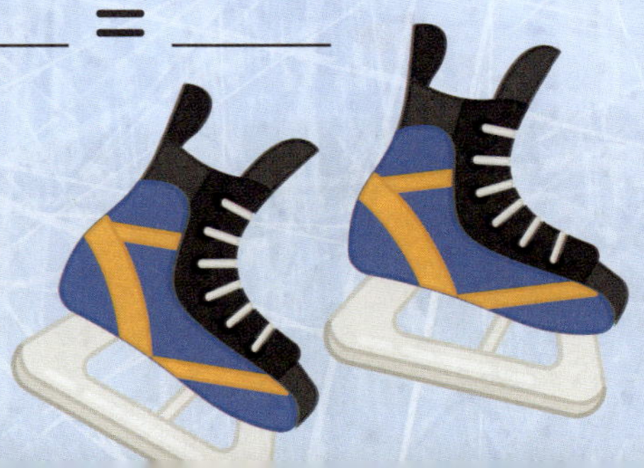

Time for Sports

# A Great Shot

**Skill:**
Add and subtract two-digit numbers

Add or subtract the **ones** first.
Then add or subtract the **tens**.

| tens | ones |
|---|---|
| 2 | 7 |
| + 3 | 0 |
| 5 | 7 |

start on the ones side

| tens | ones |
|---|---|
| 9 | 8 |
| − 2 | 5 |
| | |

| tens | ones |
|---|---|
| 1 | 3 |
| + 3 | 1 |
| | |

| tens | ones |
|---|---|
| 6 | 4 |
| − 3 | 0 |
| | |

| tens | ones |
|---|---|
| 6 | 0 |
| + 2 | 5 |
| | |

| tens | ones |
|---|---|
| 3 | 7 |
| − 2 | 7 |
| | |

| tens | ones |
|---|---|
| 8 | 6 |
| − 7 | 5 |
| | |

| tens | ones |
|---|---|
| 7 | 1 |
| − 5 | 1 |
| | |

| tens | ones |
|---|---|
| 5 | 1 |
| + 4 | 4 |
| | |

Time for Sports

**Skills:**
Use addition strategies (regrouping); Add two-digit numbers

Sometimes you get an extra ten when you add ones.
Circle the extra ten. Write it. Then add the tens and ones.

**EXAMPLE**

$$\begin{array}{r} 26 \\ +\ 8 \\ \hline \end{array}$$

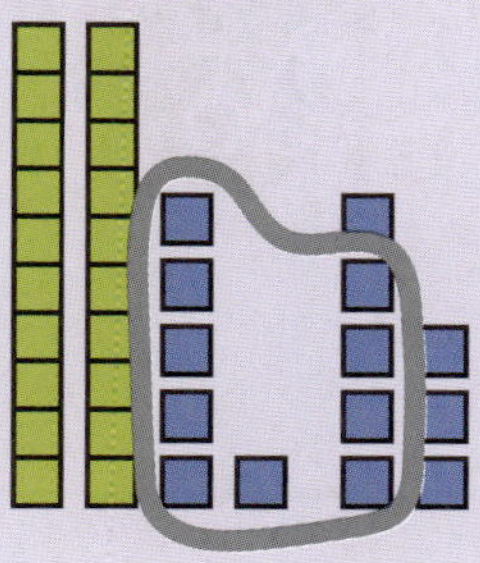

20 + 10 + 4 = 34

$$\begin{array}{r} 17 \\ +\ 6 \\ \hline \end{array}$$

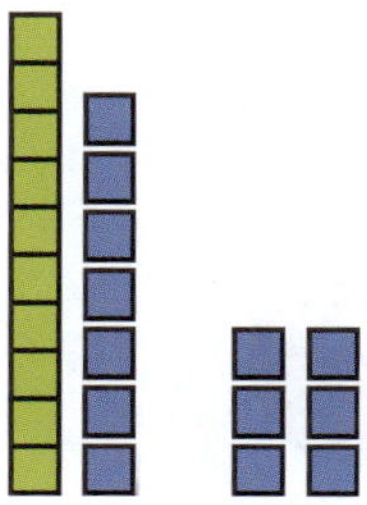

____ + ____ + ____ = ____

$$\begin{array}{r} 45 \\ +\ 9 \\ \hline \end{array}$$

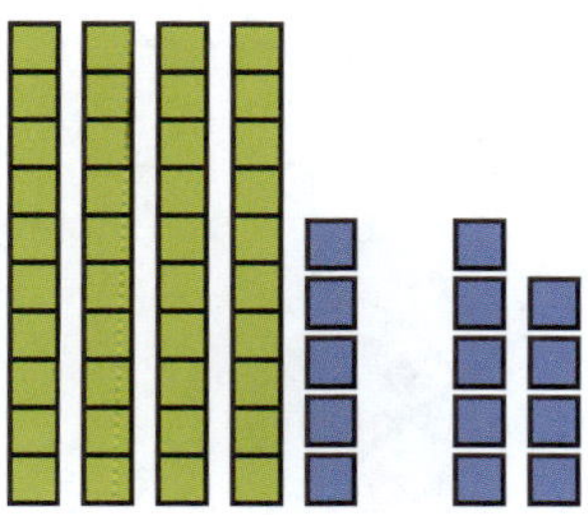

____ + ____ + ____ = ____

$$\begin{array}{r} 29 \\ +\ 7 \\ \hline \end{array}$$

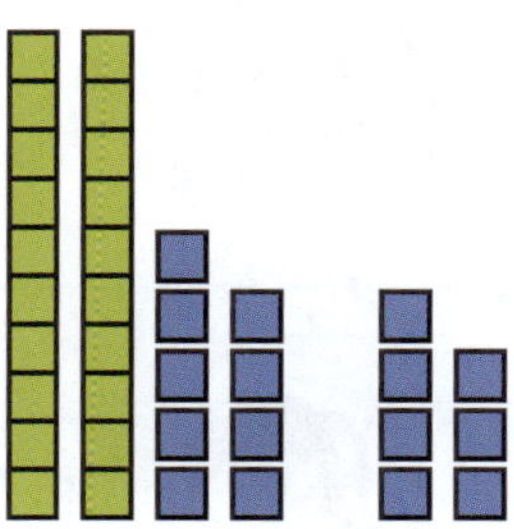

____ + ____ + ____ = ____

Time for Sports

# All Kinds of Sports

Note: You may need to help your child read the word problems.

**Skills:**
Solve word problems;
Use addition strategies (regrouping);
Add two-digit numbers

Read. Write the problems. Solve them.

The store has 23 baseball caps and 15 football helmets. How many caps and helmets are there in all?

There are _____ caps and helmets in all.

---

Lily made 15 baskets. Joy made 9 baskets. How many baskets did Lily and Joy make for the team?

Lily and Joy made _____ baskets for the team.

---

Quinn shot 19 arrows at a round target. Then he shot 8 arrows at a square target. How many arrows did he shoot in all?

Quinn shot _____ arrows in all.

---

Damian ran 14 laps this morning and 12 laps this afternoon. How many laps did Damian run today?

Damian ran _____ laps today.

**Skill:** Count by 5s

Help the family get to the sports stadium. Count by 5s to 100. Write the numbers on the road.

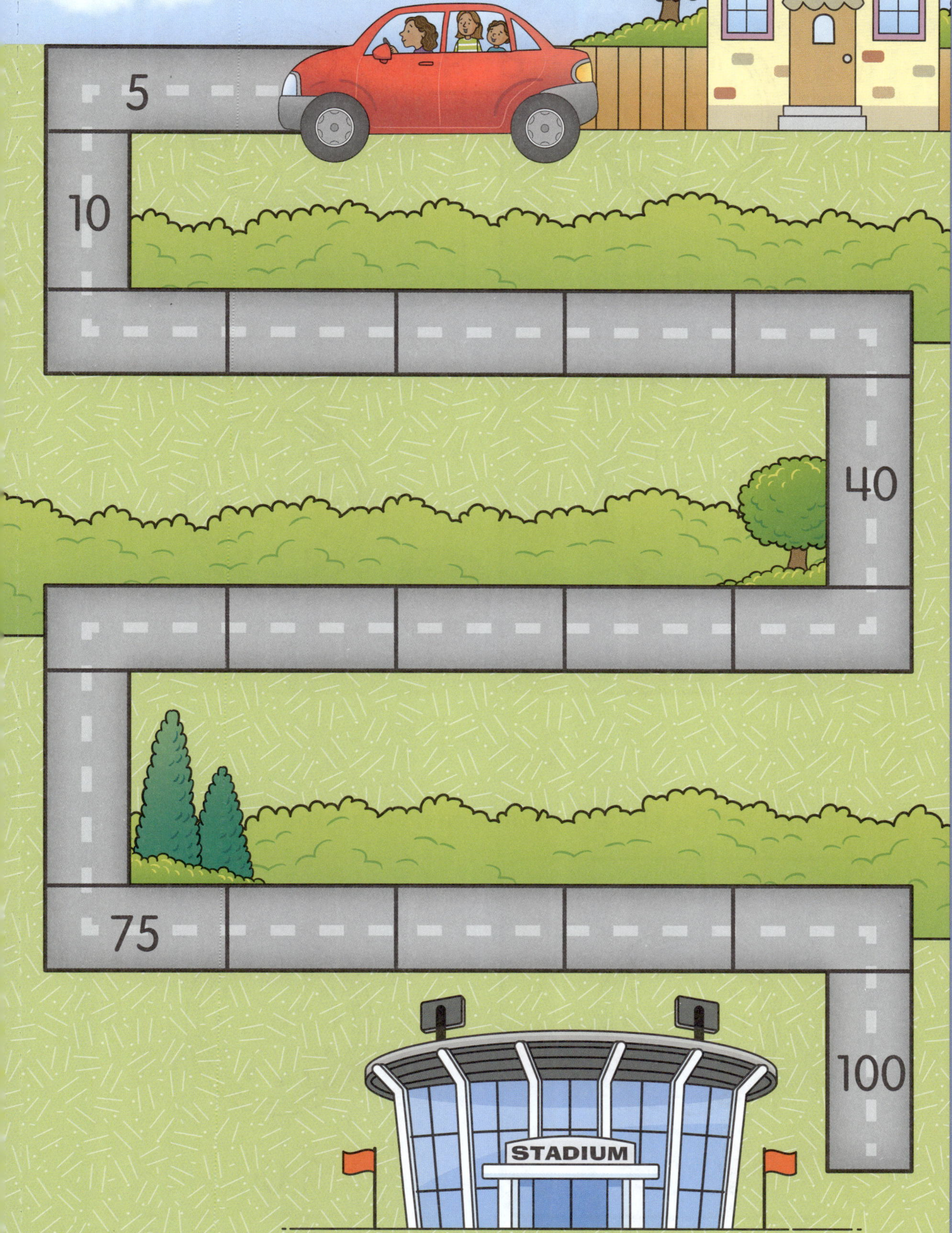

# Let the Games Begin!

**Skill:**
Tell time to the half hour

Time for Sports

Write the time that each game will start.

**Soccer Game**

_____ : _____

**Baseball Game**

_____ : _____

**Hockey Game**

_____ : _____

**Basketball Game**

_____ : _____

Draw hands on the clock to show when each game starts.

**Golf Game**

12:00

**Tennis Match**

9:00

Dylan, Kelly, Mia, and Lin will play basketball today. The table shows when their teams will practice.

| Practice Schedule | |
|---|---|
| Dylan's Team | 1:00 |
| Kelly's Team | 1:30 |
| Mia's Team | 2:30 |
| Lin's Team | 4:00 |

**Skill:**
Read a data table

Use the table to answer the questions.

Who will play basketball first? ____________

Who will practice at 2:30? ____________

What time is the last practice? ____________

Who will practice after Mia? ____________

What time will Kelly practice? ____________

Will Mia start before or after 3:00? ____________

# At the Sports Store

**Skill:**
Read a graph



Use the graph to answer the questions.

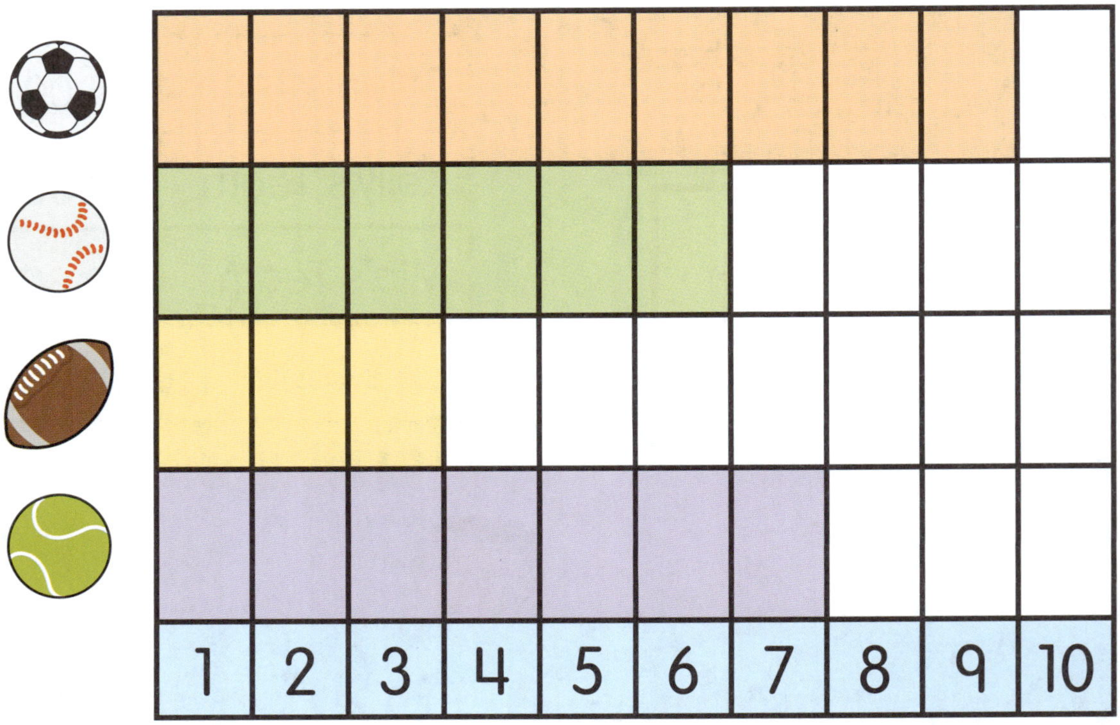


How many?

Write a question about the graph.

________________________________________

________________________________________

Write the answer to your question.

________________________________________

________________________________________

# Which Sport Do You Like Best?

**Skill:**
Read a tally

Mr. Tran's class picked the sport they liked best.
Look at the chart. Count the tally marks.

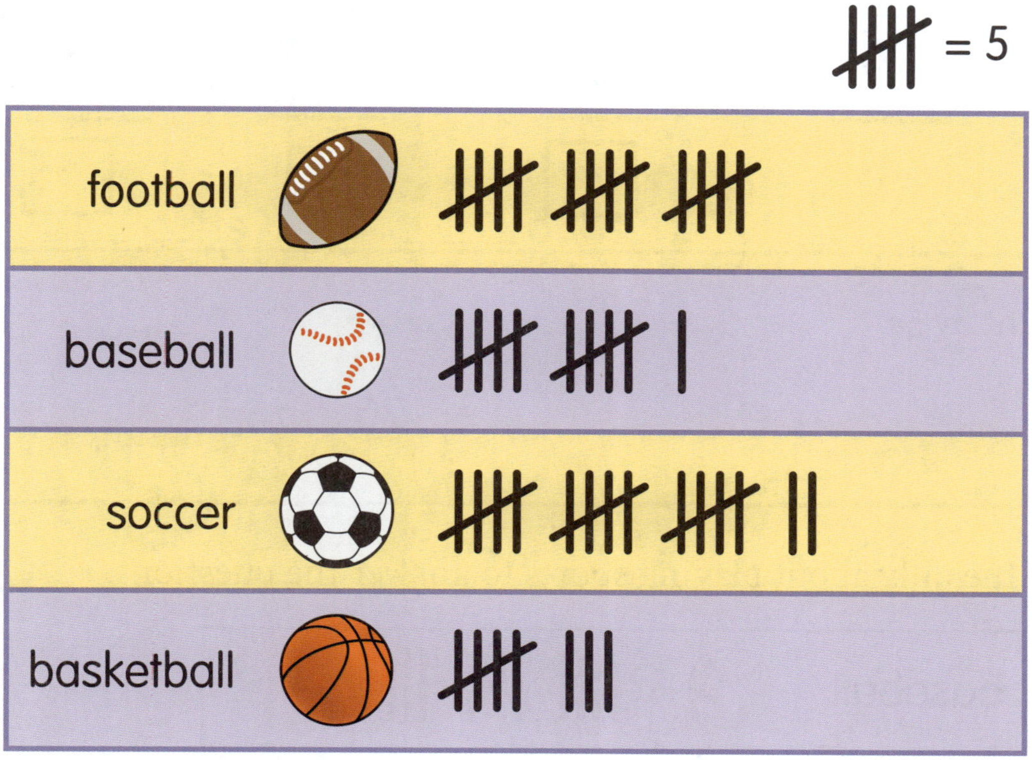


Answer the questions.

Which sports are listed on the chart?

______________________________________________

Which sport was picked the most? ____________________

Which sport was picked the least? ____________________

How many children picked football? _____

Make a red tally mark by the sport you like best.

TEST YOUR SKILLS

Time for Sports

Add.

| | | | |
|---|---|---|---|
| 5 | | □ | |
| □ | 26 | 3 | 55 |
| + 2 | + 5 | + 2 | + 34 |
| 8 | □ | 11 | □ |

Count by 5s.

35, _____, _____, _____        70, _____, _____, _____

Use the tally about playing sports to answer the questions.

| | | |
|---|---|---|
| baseball | ⚾ | 𝍸 𝍸 \|\|\| |
| soccer | ⚽ | 𝍸 𝍸 𝍸 |

𝍸 = 5

How many children play baseball? _____

How many children play soccer? _____

Read. Answer the questions.

Keisha made 14 baskets. Devon made 9 baskets.

How many baskets did they make in all? _____ baskets

How many more baskets did Keisha make than Devon?

_____ more

# You're a Math Star!

Name

completed

*Skill Sharpeners: Math*

# Answer Key

## Page 6

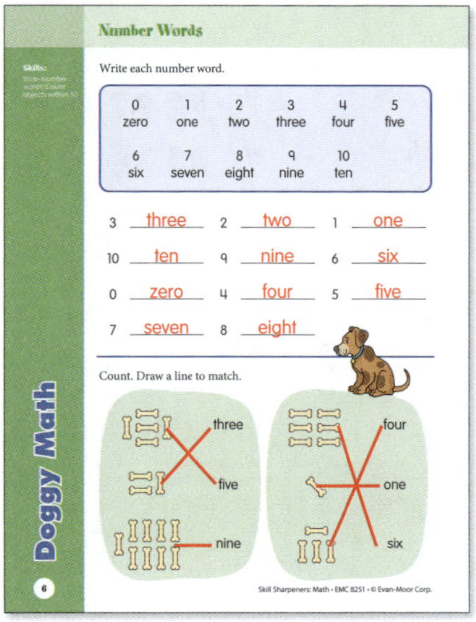
Number Words

Write each number word.

0 zero, 1 one, 2 two, 3 three, 4 four, 5 five, 6 six, 7 seven, 8 eight, 9 nine, 10 ten

3 three · 2 two · 1 one
10 ten · 9 nine · 6 six
0 zero · 4 four · 5 five
7 seven · 8 eight

Count. Draw a line to match.

three · five · nine · four · one · six

Doggy Math

6

Skill Sharpeners: Math • EMC 8251 • © Evan-Moor Corp.

## Page 7

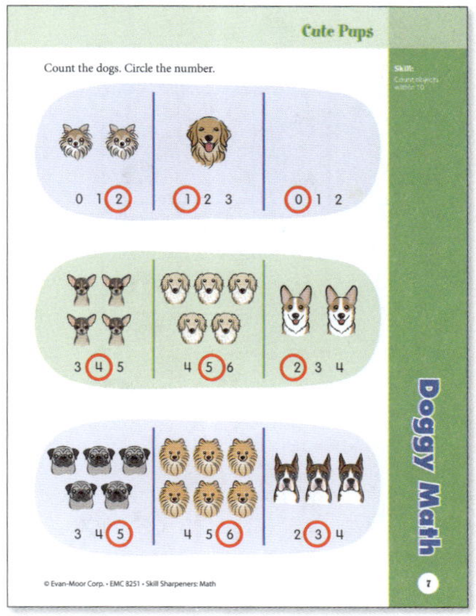
Cute Pups

Count the dogs. Circle the number.

0 1 (2) · (1) 2 3 · (0) 1 2
3 (4) 5 · 4 (5) 6 · (2) 3 4
3 4 (5) · 4 5 (6) · 2 (3) 4

Doggy Math

7

© Evan-Moor Corp. • EMC 8251 • Skill Sharpeners: Math

## Page 8

Find the Doghouse

Count. Draw lines to match the dogs to their houses.

3 · 4 · 5 · 6 · 7 · 8

Doggy Math

8

Skill Sharpeners: Math • EMC 8251 • © Evan-Moor Corp.

## Page 9

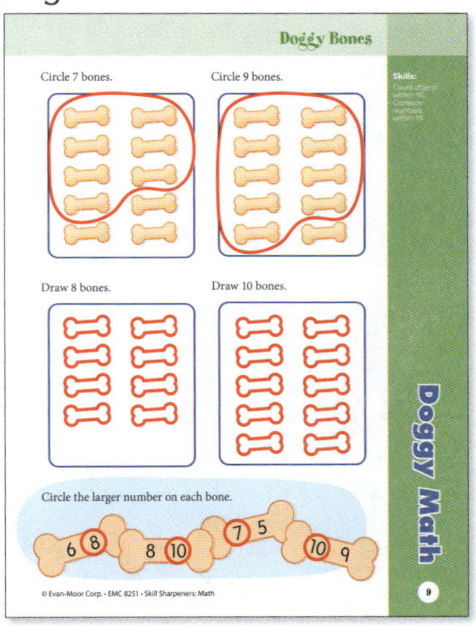
Doggy Bones

Circle 7 bones. · Circle 9 bones.

Draw 8 bones. · Draw 10 bones.

Circle the larger number on each bone.

6 (8) · 8 (10) · (7) 5 · (10) 9

Doggy Math

9

© Evan-Moor Corp. • EMC 8251 • Skill Sharpeners: Math

## Page 10

Count and Tell

How many legs? has 4 legs.

How many ears? has 2 ears.

How many feet in all? and have 8 feet in all.

How many bones? has 9 bones.

Which answer is the largest? 9

Which answer is the smallest? 2

Doggy Math

10

Skill Sharpeners: Math • EMC 8251 • © Evan-Moor Corp.

## Page 11

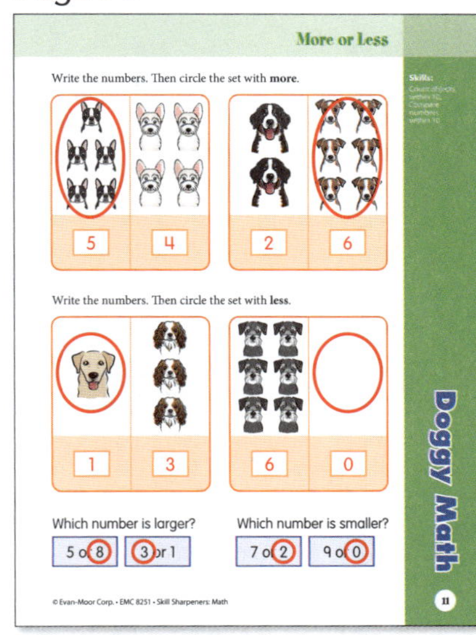
More or Less

Write the numbers. Then circle the set with more.

5 · 4 · 2 · 6

Write the numbers. Then circle the set with less.

1 · 3 · 6 · 0

Which number is larger? 5 or (8) · (3) or 1

Which number is smaller? 7 or (2) · 9 or (0)

Doggy Math

11

© Evan-Moor Corp. • EMC 8251 • Skill Sharpeners: Math

## Page 12

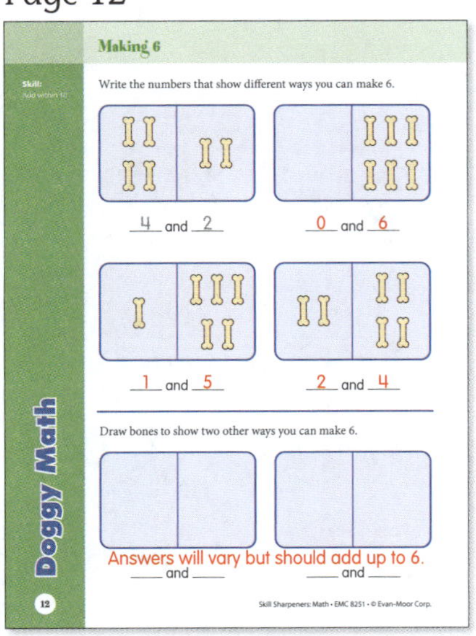
Making 6

Write the numbers that show different ways you can make 6.

4 and 2 · 0 and 6
1 and 5 · 2 and 4

Draw bones to show two other ways you can make 6.

Answers will vary but should add up to 6.
___ and ___ · ___ and ___

Doggy Math

12

Skill Sharpeners: Math • EMC 8251 • © Evan-Moor Corp.

## Page 13

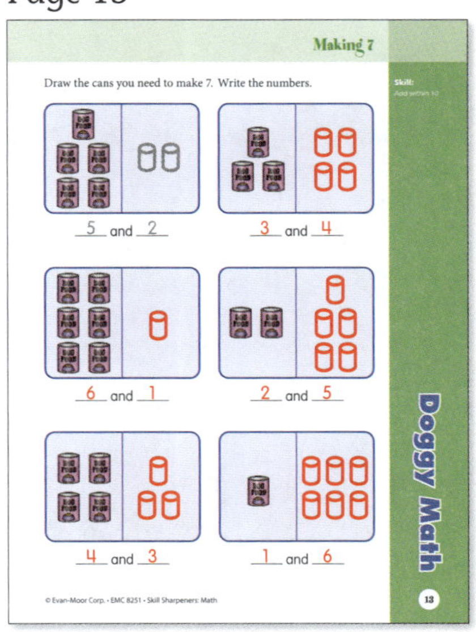
Making 7

Draw the cans you need to make 7. Write the numbers.

5 and 2 · 3 and 4
6 and 1 · 2 and 5
4 and 3 · 1 and 6

Doggy Math

13

© Evan-Moor Corp. • EMC 8251 • Skill Sharpeners: Math

## Page 14

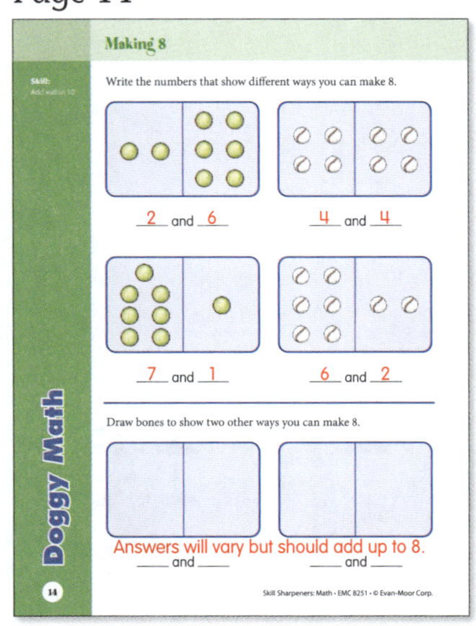
Making 8

Write the numbers that show different ways you can make 8.

2 and 6 · 4 and 4
7 and 1 · 6 and 2

Draw bones to show two other ways you can make 8.

Answers will vary but should add up to 8.
___ and ___ · ___ and ___

Doggy Math

14

Skill Sharpeners: Math • EMC 8251 • © Evan-Moor Corp.

Page 15

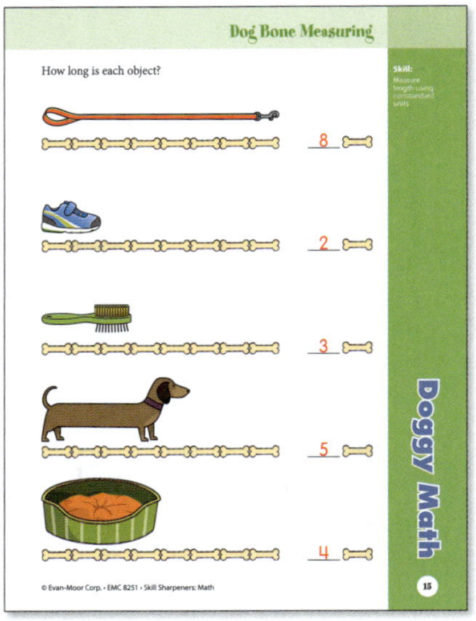
Dog Bone Measuring

How long is each object?

8
2
3
5
4

Doggy Math

15

© Evan-Moor Corp. • EMC 8251 • Skill Sharpeners: Math

Page 16

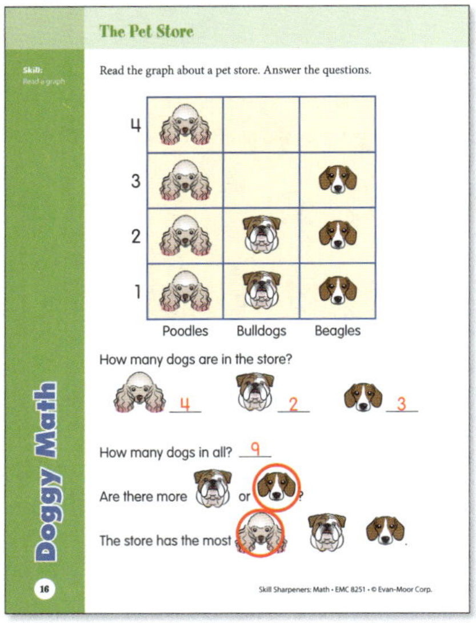
The Pet Store

Read the graph about a pet store. Answer the questions.

4
3
2
1
Poodles Bulldogs Beagles

How many dogs are in the store?
4 2 3

How many dogs in all? 9

Are there more or ?

The store has the most

Doggy Math

16

Skill Sharpeners: Math • EMC 8251 • © Evan-Moor Corp.

Page 17

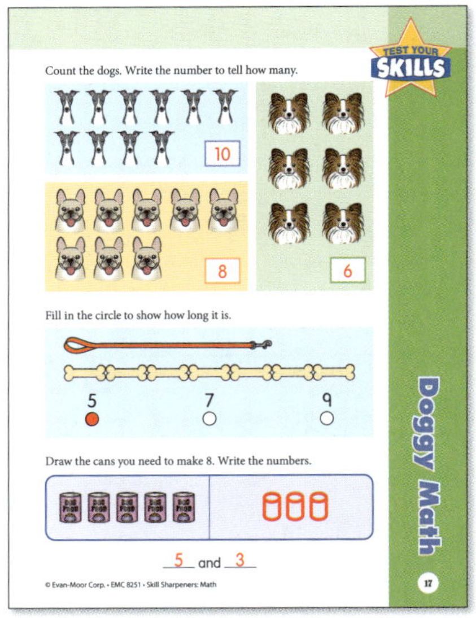
TEST YOUR SKILLS

Count the dogs. Write the number to tell how many.

10
8
6

Fill in the circle to show how long it is.

5 7 9

Draw the cans you need to make 8. Write the numbers.

5 and 3

Doggy Math

17

© Evan-Moor Corp. • EMC 8251 • Skill Sharpeners: Math

Page 18

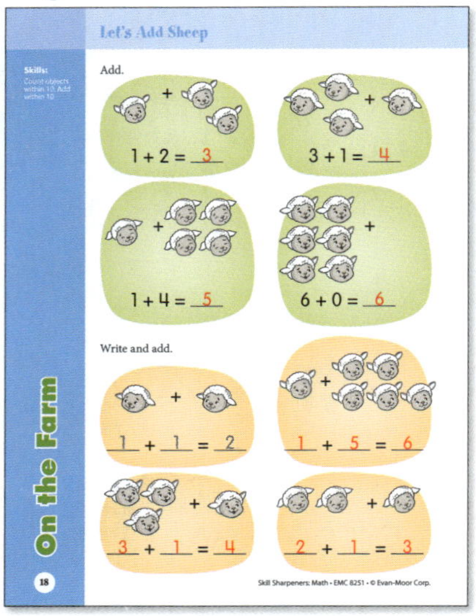
Let's Add Sheep

Add.

1 + 2 = 3
3 + 1 = 4
1 + 4 = 5
6 + 0 = 6

Write and add.

1 + 1 = 2
1 + 5 = 6
3 + 1 = 4
2 + 1 = 3

On the Farm

18

Skill Sharpeners: Math • EMC 8251 • © Evan-Moor Corp.

Page 19

Note: You may need to help your child read the word problems.

Animals on the Farm

Add.

There are 2 horses.
2 more horses come.
How many horses now?
2 + 2 = 4
4 horses

There are 3 sheep.
3 more sheep come.
How many sheep now?
3 + 3 = 6
6 sheep

There are 0 hens.
5 hens come.
How many hens now?
0 + 5 = 5
5 hens

There are 2 goats.
1 more goat comes.
How many goats now?
2 + 1 = 3
3 goats

On the Farm

19

© Evan-Moor Corp. • EMC 8251 • Skill Sharpeners: Math

Page 20

Playful Sheep

Add.

2 + 2 = 4 3 + 2 = 5 4 + 2 = 6
1 + 2 = 3 0 + 2 = 2 1 + 1 = 2
3 + 1 = 4 1 + 0 = 1 0 + 3 = 3
0 + 0 = 0 2 + 3 = 5 3 + 3 = 6

3 + 1 = 4
2 + 3 = 5
0 + 3 = 3
3 + 3 = 6
0 + 0 = 0

1 + 0 = 1
4 + 2 = 6
4 + 1 = 5
2 + 2 = 4
1 + 1 = 2

On the Farm

20

Skill Sharpeners: Math • EMC 8251 • © Evan-Moor Corp.

Page 21

The Answer Is the Same

Add.

3 + 2 = 5 0 + 1 = 1 1 + 2 = 3
2 + 3 = 5 1 + 0 = 1 2 + 1 = 3
0 + 4 = 4 1 + 5 = 6 0 + 6 = 6
4 + 0 = 4 5 + 1 = 6 6 + 0 = 6
3 + 0 = 3 3 + 1 = 4 4 + 2 = 6
0 + 3 = 3 1 + 3 = 4 2 + 4 = 6

Write two addition problems for each cow.

EXAMPLE
1, 2, 3
1 + 2 = 3
2 + 1 = 3

2, 3, 5
2 + 3 = 5
3 + 2 = 5

1, 5, 6
1 + 5 = 6
5 + 1 = 6

On the Farm

21

© Evan-Moor Corp. • EMC 8251 • Skill Sharpeners: Math

Page 22

How Many Chicks?

Subtract.

3 − 2 = 1
5 − 3 = 2
4 − 0 = 4
6 − 4 = 2

Write and subtract.

5 − 1 = 4
3 − 3 = 0
4 − 1 = 3
6 − 3 = 3

On the Farm

22

Skill Sharpeners: Math • EMC 8251 • © Evan-Moor Corp.

Page 23

Note: You may need to help your child read the word problems.

Animals Go Away

Subtract.

There are 5 hens.
1 hen goes away.
How many hens now?
5 − 1 = 4
4 hens

There are 4 cows.
2 cows go away.
How many cows now?
4 − 2 = 2
2 cows

There are 6 chicks.
2 chicks go away.
How many chicks now?
6 − 2 = 4
4 chicks

There are 5 horses.
3 horses go away.
How many horses now?
5 − 3 = 2
2 horses

On the Farm

23

© Evan-Moor Corp. • EMC 8251 • Skill Sharpeners: Math

Page 24

Page 25

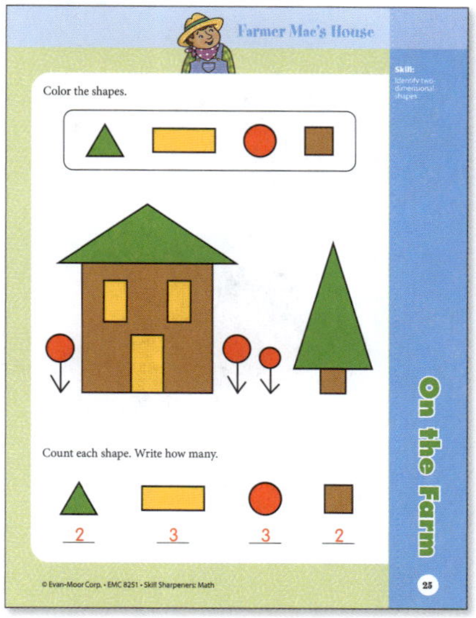


Page 26

Page 27

Page 28

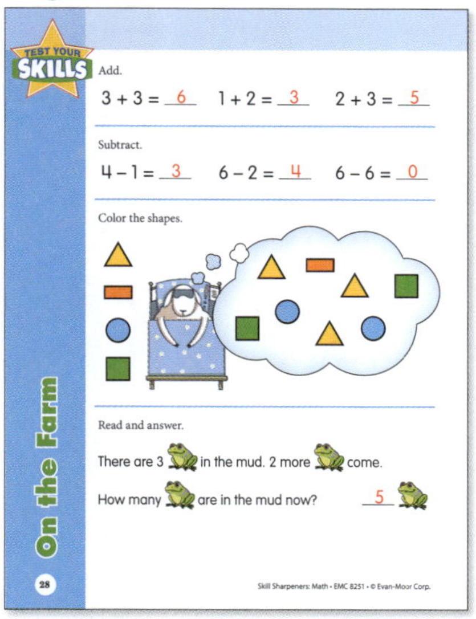


Page 29

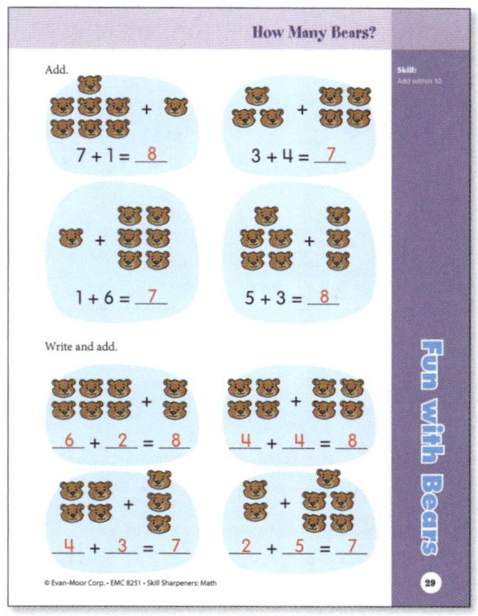


Page 30

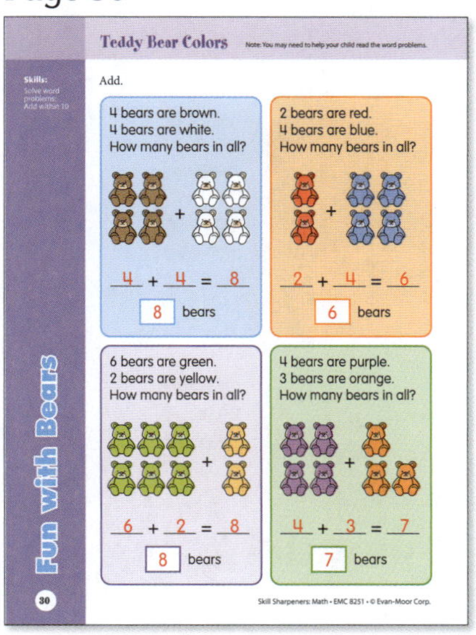


Page 31

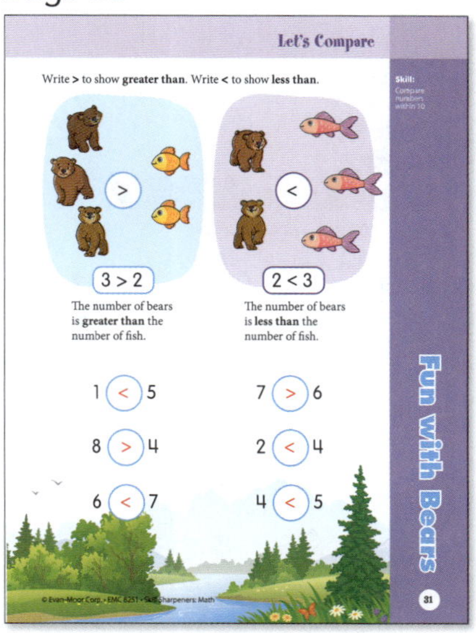


Page 32

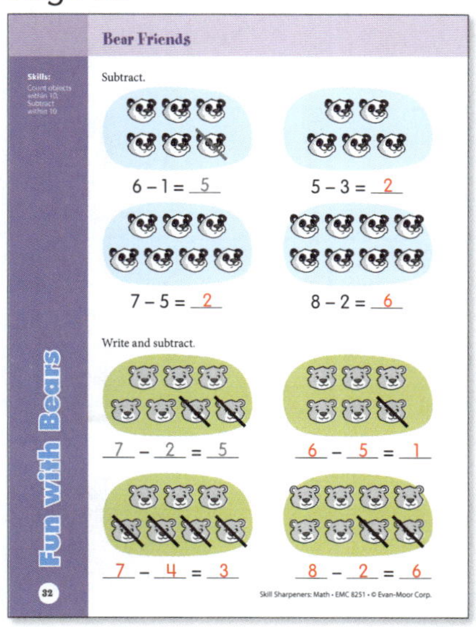

Page 33

**Hungry Bears**

Note: You may need to help your child read the word problems.

Read. Write the problems. Solve them.

Black Bear had 7 berries. He ate 3 berries. How many berries were left? 7 − 3 = 4. 4 berries were left.

6 baby bears were in a tree. 1 climbed down. How many baby bears were still in the tree? 6 − 1 = 5. 5 baby bears were still in the tree.

Grizzly Bear caught 8 fish. 1 swam away. How many fish were left? 8 − 1 = 7. 7 fish were left.

Sun Bear had 7 nuts. Sun Bear ate 5 of them. How many nuts were left? 7 − 5 = 2. 2 nuts were left.

Skill: Solve word problems; Subtract within 10

Fun with Bears

© Evan-Moor Corp. • EMC 8251 • Skill Sharpeners: Math • 33

Page 34

**Color the Bear**

Skill: Subtract within 10

Subtract. Color.

orange 0; brown 1; blue 2; red 3; green 4; purple 5; yellow 6



Subtract.

6 − 6 = 0   3 − 3 = 0   4 − 4 = 0

8 − 8 = 0   5 − 5 = 0   2 − 2 = 0

When you subtract a number from itself, you get 0.

Fun with Bears

34 • Skill Sharpeners: Math • EMC 8251 • © Evan-Moor Corp.

Page 35

**Bears at Play**

Skill: Add and subtract within 10

Add.

2 + 3 = 5   4 + 4 = 8   6 + 1 = 7

4 + 2 = 6   2 + 5 = 7   5 + 3 = 8

Subtract.

6 − 6 = 0   8 − 1 = 7   7 − 5 = 2

5 − 3 = 2   7 − 3 = 4   8 − 2 = 6

Add or subtract.

3 + 3 = 6   6 + 2 = 8   5 + 0 = 5   4 + 3 = 7   2 + 6 = 8

6 − 2 = 4   7 − 1 = 6   8 − 8 = 0   5 − 2 = 3   8 − 6 = 2

Fun with Bears

© Evan-Moor Corp. • EMC 8251 • Skill Sharpeners: Math • 35

Page 36

**In the Woods**

Skill: Measure length using inches

How many inches?

The berry is 1 inch wide.

The hive is 2 inches wide.

The fish is 3 inches long.

The flower is 1 inch wide.

The baby bear is 4 inches long.

Fun with Bears

36 • Skill Sharpeners: Math • EMC 8251 • © Evan-Moor Corp.

Page 37

**Bear Watching**

Skill: Read a graph

Read the graph. Answer the questions.

How many (brown bears)? 4

How many (pandas)? 6

How many more (pandas) than (black bears)? 3 more

How many more (brown bears) than (polar bears)? 3 more

How many more (pandas) than (polar bears)? 5 more

Fun with Bears

© Evan-Moor Corp. • EMC 8251 • Skill Sharpeners: Math • 37

Page 38

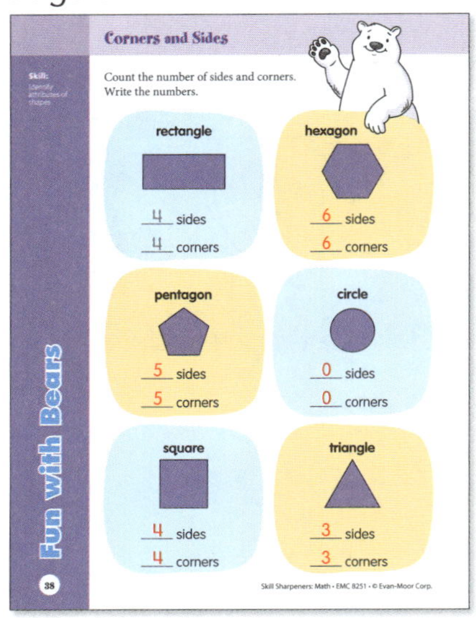

**Corners and Sides**

Skill: Identify attributes of shapes

Count the number of sides and corners. Write the numbers.

rectangle: 4 sides, 4 corners

hexagon: 6 sides, 6 corners

pentagon: 5 sides, 5 corners

circle: 0 sides, 0 corners

square: 4 sides, 4 corners

triangle: 3 sides, 3 corners

Fun with Bears

38 • Skill Sharpeners: Math • EMC 8251 • © Evan-Moor Corp.

Page 39

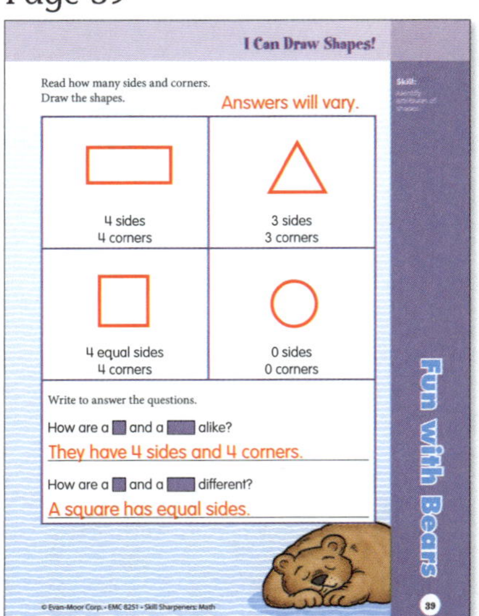

**I Can Draw Shapes!**

Skill: Identify attributes of shapes

Read how many sides and corners. Draw the shapes.

Answers will vary.

4 sides, 4 corners

3 sides, 3 corners

4 equal sides, 4 corners

0 sides, 0 corners

Write to answer the questions.

How are a (square) and a (rectangle) alike? They have 4 sides and 4 corners.

How are a (square) and a (rectangle) different? A square has equal sides.

Fun with Bears

© Evan-Moor Corp. • EMC 8251 • Skill Sharpeners: Math • 39

Page 40

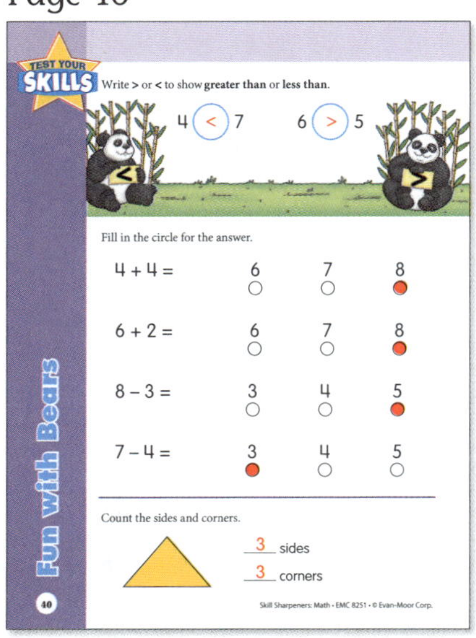

**Test Your Skills**

Write > or < to show greater than or less than.

4 < 7   6 > 5

Fill in the circle for the answer.

4 + 4 = 6, 7, 8 (8)

6 + 2 = 6, 7, 8 (8)

8 − 3 = 3, 4, 5 (5)

7 − 4 = 3, 4, 5 (3)

Count the sides and corners.

3 sides, 3 corners

Fun with Bears

40 • Skill Sharpeners: Math • EMC 8251 • © Evan-Moor Corp.

Page 41

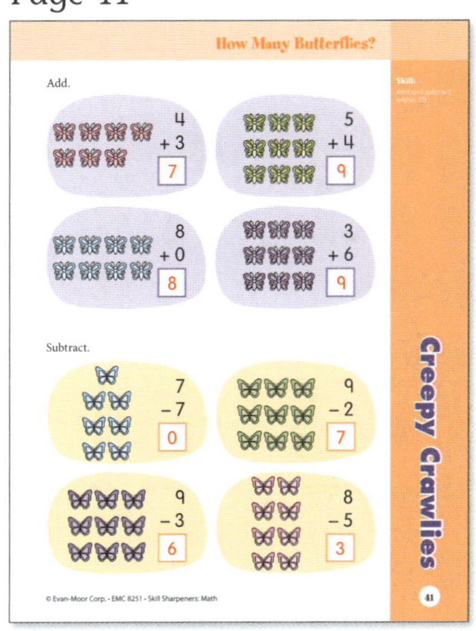

**How Many Butterflies?**

Skill: Add and subtract within 10

Add.

4 + 3 = 7   5 + 4 = 9

8 + 0 = 8   3 + 6 = 9

Subtract.

7 − 7 = 0   9 − 2 = 7

9 − 3 = 6   8 − 5 = 3

Creepy Crawlies

© Evan-Moor Corp. • EMC 8251 • Skill Sharpeners: Math • 41

## Page 42

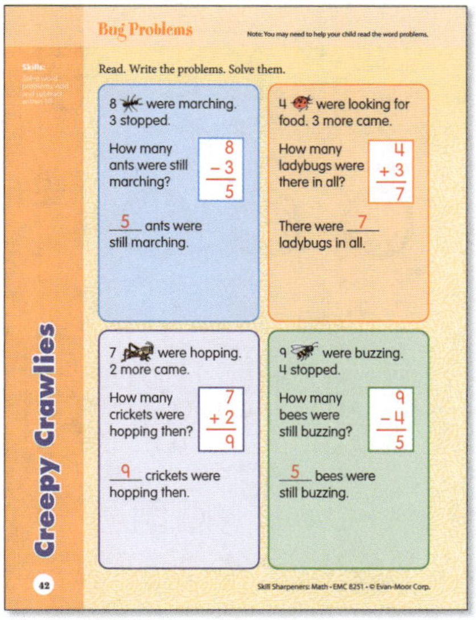

Bug Problems

Note: You may need to help your child read the word problems.

Read. Write the problems. Solve them.

8 ants were marching. 3 stopped. How many ants were still marching? 8 − 3 = 5. 5 ants were still marching.

4 ladybugs were looking for food. 3 more came. How many ladybugs were there in all? 4 + 3 = 7. There were 7 ladybugs in all.

7 crickets were hopping. 2 more came. How many crickets were hopping then? 7 + 2 = 9. 9 crickets were hopping then.

9 bees were buzzing. 4 stopped. How many bees were still buzzing? 9 − 4 = 5. 5 bees were still buzzing.

## Page 43

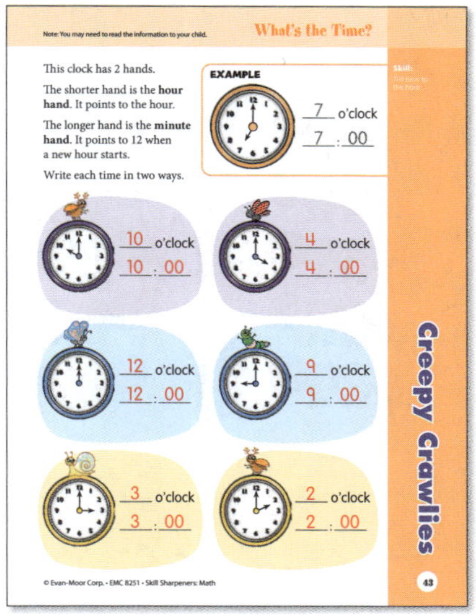

What's the Time?

Note: You may need to read the information to your child.

This clock has 2 hands. The shorter hand is the **hour hand**. It points to the hour. The longer hand is the **minute hand**. It points to 12 when a new hour starts.

Write each time in two ways.

EXAMPLE: 7 o'clock, 7 : 00

10 o'clock, 10 : 00 — 4 o'clock, 4 : 00 — 12 o'clock, 12 : 00 — 9 o'clock, 9 : 00 — 3 o'clock, 3 : 00 — 2 o'clock, 2 : 00

## Page 44

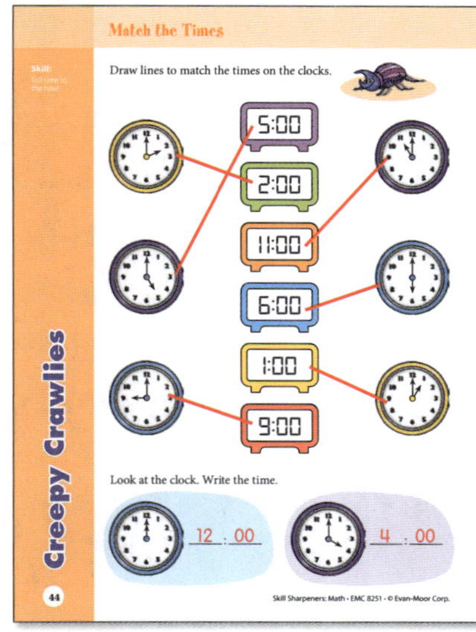

Match the Times

Draw lines to match the times on the clocks.

5:00, 2:00, 11:00, 6:00, 1:00, 9:00

Look at the clock. Write the time.

12 : 00 — 4 : 00

## Page 45

Busy Ants

Write two addition problems and two subtraction problems.

6, 3, 9: 6 + 3 = 9; 3 + 6 = 9; 9 − 3 = 6; 9 − 6 = 3

7, 2, 9: 9 − 2 = 7; 9 − 7 = 2; 7 + 2 = 9; 2 + 7 = 9

7, 3, 10: 7 + 3 = 10; 3 + 7 = 10; 10 − 3 = 7; 10 − 7 = 3

8, 2, 10: 10 − 2 = 8; 10 − 8 = 2; 8 + 2 = 10; 2 + 8 = 10

Mark ☒ the one that does **not** belong in the family of facts.

1 + 7 = 8 — 7 + 1 = 8 — 8 − 1 = 7 — 7 − 1 = 6 ☒

Write the missing fact from this family.

8 − 7 = 1

## Page 46

What's Missing?

Write the numbers.

7 + 0 = 7 — 2 + 8 = 10 — 1 + 8 = 9 — 4 + 4 = 8 — 8 − 8 = 0 — 9 − 4 = 5 — 6 − 2 = 4 — 9 − 6 = 3 — 4 + 6 = 10

## Page 47

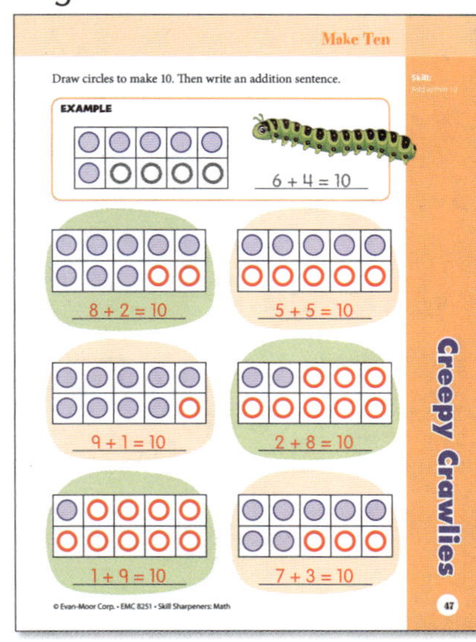

Make Ten

Draw circles to make 10. Then write an addition sentence.

EXAMPLE: 6 + 4 = 10

8 + 2 = 10 — 5 + 5 = 10 — 9 + 1 = 10 — 2 + 8 = 10 — 1 + 9 = 10 — 7 + 3 = 10

## Page 48

Ladybugs Are Everywhere!

Add or subtract. Color the ladybugs that = 6.

4 + 5, 5 + 1, 2 + 4, 8 − 2, 6 − 1, 7 − 2, 10 − 4, 7 + 1, 9 − 3

Add or subtract. Color the ladybugs that = 7.

5 + 2, 6 + 2, 9 − 2, 8 − 5, 6 − 3, 1 + 6, 3 + 5, 10 − 3, 2 + 6

## Page 49

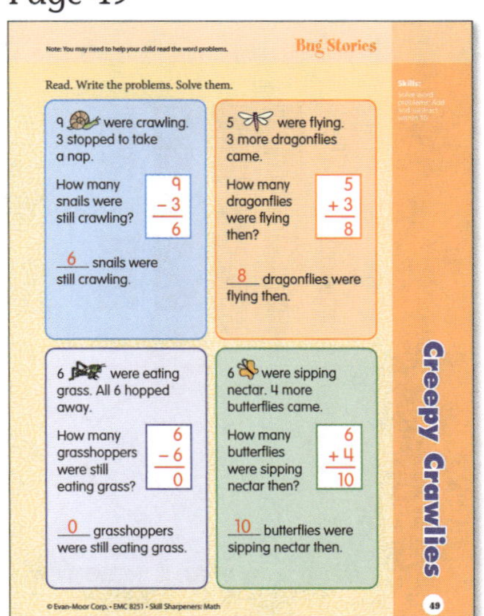

Bug Stories

Note: You may need to help your child read the word problems.

Read. Write the problems. Solve them.

9 snails were crawling. 3 stopped to take a nap. How many snails were still crawling? 9 − 3 = 6. 6 snails were still crawling.

5 dragonflies were flying. 3 more dragonflies came. How many dragonflies were flying then? 5 + 3 = 8. 8 dragonflies were flying then.

6 grasshoppers were eating grass. All 6 hopped away. How many grasshoppers were still eating grass? 6 − 6 = 0. 0 grasshoppers were still eating grass.

6 butterflies were sipping nectar. 4 more butterflies came. How many butterflies were sipping nectar then? 6 + 4 = 10. 10 butterflies were sipping nectar then.

## Page 50

Garden Friends

Look at the grass. Count how many. Color the graph to show how many.

There are the most — ladybug (circled)

There are the least — butterfly (circled)

Which 2 have the same number? — bee and snail (circled)

Page 51

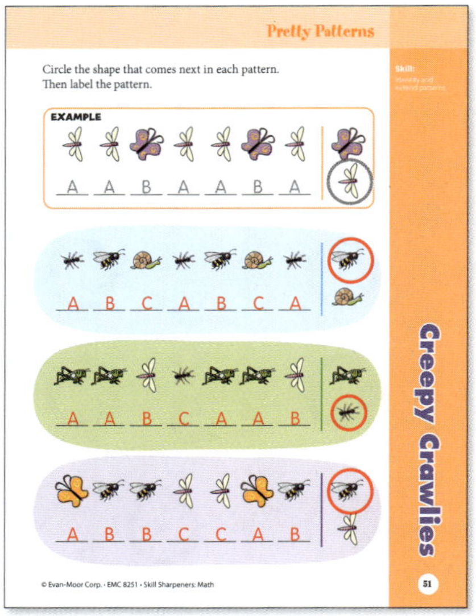
Pretty Patterns

Skill: Identify and extend patterns

Circle the shape that comes next in each pattern. Then label the pattern.

EXAMPLE

A A B A A B A

A B C A B C A

A A B C A A B

A B B C C A B

Creepy Crawlies

© Evan-Moor Corp. • EMC 8251 • Skill Sharpeners: Math

51

Page 52

Hungry Caterpillars

Skill: Add and subtract within 10

Find the answers. Draw a line from each caterpillar to the flower with the correct answer.

8 − 4, 9 − 8, 4 + 2, 10 − 8, 7 − 2

1, 2, 3, 4, 5, 6

6 − 3, 9 − 4, 3 + 3, 10 − 9, 8 − 6

Draw a picture to show each number sentence. Write the answer.

Pictures will vary.

5 + 5 = 10 | 9 − 7 = 2 | 3 + 6 = 9

Creepy Crawlies

52

Skill Sharpeners: Math • EMC 8251 • © Evan-Moor Corp.

Page 53

TEST YOUR SKILLS

Add or subtract.

3 + 5 = 8    6 + 2 = 8    9 − 6 = 3

7 − 4 = 3    3 + 7 = 10    10 − 1 = 9

Write the time in two ways.

2 o'clock    9 o'clock    6 o'clock

2 : 00    9 : 00    6 : 00

Draw circles to make 10. Then write an addition sentence.

8 + 2 = 10    3 + 7 = 10

Finish the pattern. Then label it.

A A B C A A B C A

Creepy Crawlies

© Evan-Moor Corp. • EMC 8251 • Skill Sharpeners: Math

53

Page 54

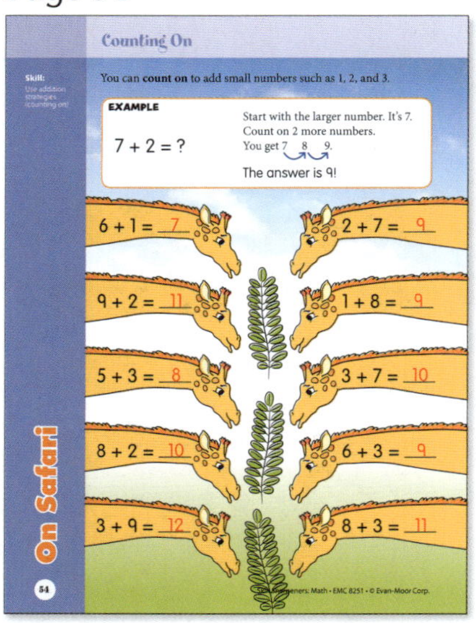
Counting On

Skill: Use addition strategies (counting on)

You can **count on** to add small numbers such as 1, 2, and 3.

EXAMPLE

7 + 2 = ?

Start with the larger number. It's 7. Count on 2 more numbers. You get 7 8 9.

The answer is 9!

6 + 1 = 7    2 + 7 = 9

9 + 2 = 11    1 + 8 = 9

5 + 3 = 8    3 + 7 = 10

8 + 2 = 10    6 + 3 = 9

3 + 9 = 12    8 + 3 = 11

On Safari

54

Skill Sharpeners: Math • EMC 8251 • © Evan-Moor Corp.

Page 55

Counting Back

Skill: Use subtraction strategies (counting back)

You can **count back** to subtract small numbers such as 1, 2, and 3.

EXAMPLE

8 − 2 = ?

Start with the first number. It's 8. Count back 2 more numbers. You get 8 7 6.

The answer is 6!

10 − 3 = 7    9 − 1 = 8

10 − 2 = 8    11 − 3 = 8

8 − 1 = 7    12 − 3 = 9

9 − 2 = 7    11 − 2 = 9

10 − 1 = 9    9 − 3 = 6

Write two more problems you can solve by counting back.

Answers will vary.

___ − ___ = ___    ___ − ___ = ___

On Safari

© Evan-Moor Corp. • EMC 8251 • Skill Sharpeners: Math

55

Page 56

Safari Animals

Note: You may need to help your child read the word problems.

Skills: Add and subtract within 20. Solve word problems

Read. Write the problems. Solve them.

6 zebras were playing. 5 more zebras came to play. How many zebras were playing then?

6 + 5 = 11

11 zebras were playing then.

12 elephants were eating. 3 elephants went away. How many elephants were left?

12 − 3 = 9

9 elephants were left.

11 lions were sleeping. Then 3 lions woke up. How many lions were still sleeping?

11 − 3 = 8

8 lions were still sleeping.

8 ostriches were running. 4 more ostriches joined them. How many ostriches were running then?

8 + 4 = 12

12 ostriches were running then.

On Safari

56

Skill Sharpeners: Math • EMC 8251 • © Evan-Moor Corp.

Page 57

Count to 100

Skill: Count within 100

Write the numbers 1 to 100 in order.

| 1 | 2 | 3 | 4 | 5 | 6 | 7 | 8 | 9 | 10 |
|---|---|---|---|---|---|---|---|---|---|
| 11 | 12 | 13 | 14 | 15 | 16 | 17 | 18 | 19 | 20 |
| 21 | 22 | 23 | 24 | 25 | 26 | 27 | 28 | 29 | 30 |
| 31 | 32 | 33 | 34 | 35 | 36 | 37 | 38 | 39 | 40 |
| 41 | 42 | 43 | 44 | 45 | 46 | 47 | 48 | 49 | 50 |
| 51 | 52 | 53 | 54 | 55 | 56 | 57 | 58 | 59 | 60 |
| 61 | 62 | 63 | 64 | 65 | 66 | 67 | 68 | 69 | 70 |
| 71 | 72 | 73 | 74 | 75 | 76 | 77 | 78 | 79 | 80 |
| 81 | 82 | 83 | 84 | 85 | 86 | 87 | 88 | 89 | 90 |
| 91 | 92 | 93 | 94 | 95 | 96 | 97 | 98 | 99 | 100 |

On Safari

© Evan-Moor Corp. • EMC 8251 • Skill Sharpeners: Math

57

Page 58

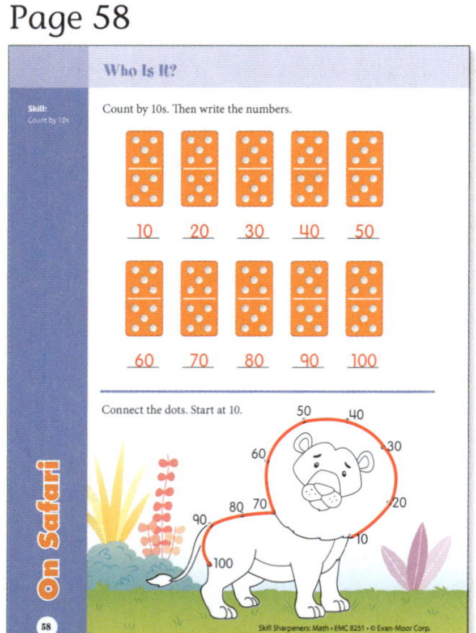
Who Is It?

Skill: Count by 10s

Count by 10s. Then write the numbers.

10 20 30 40 50

60 70 80 90 100

Connect the dots. Start at 10.

On Safari

58

Skill Sharpeners: Math • EMC 8251 • © Evan-Moor Corp.

Page 59

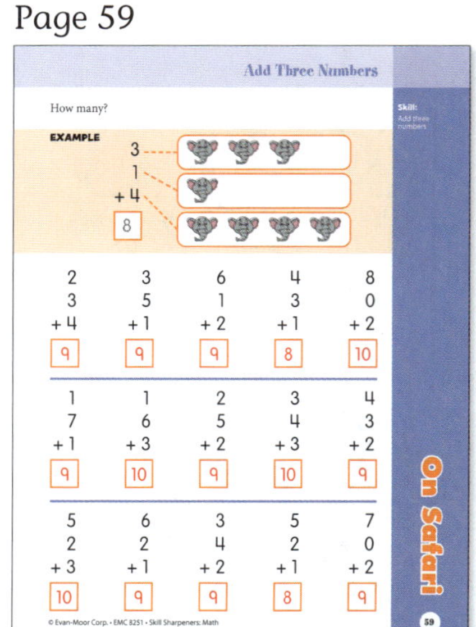
Add Three Numbers

Skill: Add three numbers

How many?

EXAMPLE

3 + 1 + 4 = 8

2 + 3 + 4 = 9    3 + 5 + 1 = 9    6 + 1 + 2 = 9    4 + 3 + 1 = 8    8 + 0 + 2 = 10

1 + 7 + 1 = 9    1 + 6 + 3 = 10    2 + 5 + 2 = 9    3 + 4 + 3 = 10    4 + 3 + 2 = 9

5 + 2 + 3 = 10    6 + 2 + 1 = 9    3 + 4 + 2 = 9    5 + 2 + 1 = 8    7 + 0 + 2 = 9

On Safari

© Evan-Moor Corp. • EMC 8251 • Skill Sharpeners: Math

59

Page 60

Mystery Boxes

Skill: Add three numbers.

Write the missing numbers.

EXAMPLE

7 →

| 2 | 3 | 2 |
|---|---|---|
| 3 | 4 | 0 |
| 2 | 0 | 5 |

2 + 3 + 2 = 7
3 + 4 + 0 = 7
2 + 0 + 5 = 7

8 →

| 3 | 2 | 3 |
|---|---|---|
| 2 | 5 | 1 |
| 3 | 1 | 4 |

9 →

| 2 | 3 | 4 |
|---|---|---|
| 2 | 5 | 2 |
| 5 | 1 | 3 |

10 →

| 2 | 3 | 5 |
|---|---|---|
| 4 | 4 | 2 |
| 4 | 3 | 3 |

On Safari

60

Skill Sharpeners: Math • EMC 8251 • © Evan-Moor Corp.

Page 61

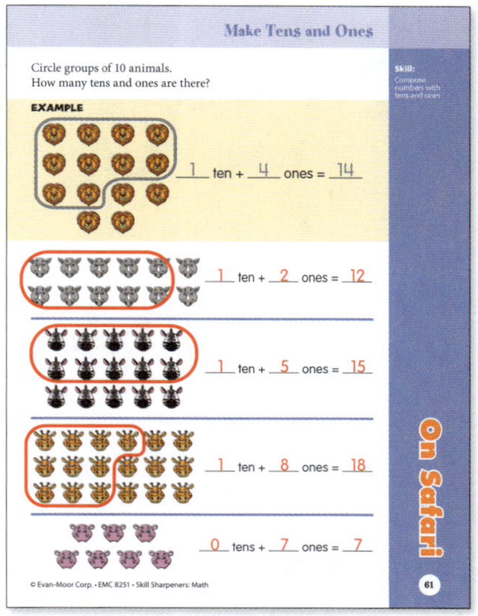
Make Tens and Ones

Skill: Compose numbers with tens and ones

Circle groups of 10 animals.
How many tens and ones are there?

EXAMPLE

1 ten + 4 ones = 14

1 ten + 2 ones = 12

1 ten + 5 ones = 15

1 ten + 8 ones = 18

0 tens + 7 ones = 7

On Safari

61

© Evan-Moor Corp. • EMC 8251 • Skill Sharpeners: Math

Page 62

Tens and Ones

Skill: Compose numbers with tens and ones

Each block is one. Here are 3 ones.

There are 10 blocks in this set. This is 1 ten.

How many?

| tens | ones | | tens | ones | | tens | ones | |
|---|---|---|---|---|---|---|---|---|
| 4 | 3 | 43 | 8 | 8 | 88 | 2 | 6 | 26 |
| 3 | 2 | 32 | 6 | 4 | 64 | 1 | 0 | 10 |

On Safari

62

Skill Sharpeners: Math • EMC 8251 • © Evan-Moor Corp.

Page 63

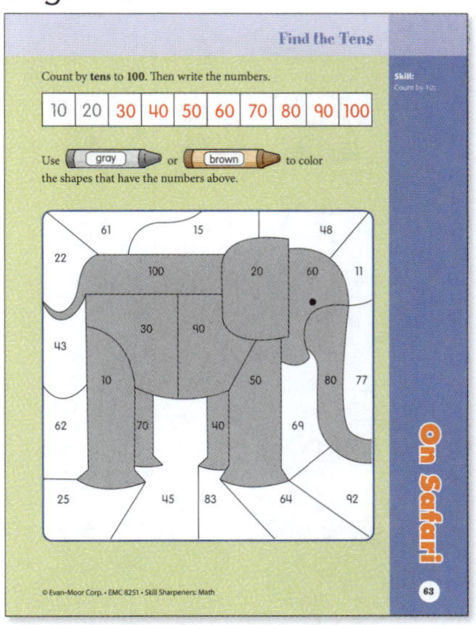
Find the Tens

Skill: Count by 10s

Count by tens to 100. Then write the numbers.

| 10 | 20 | 30 | 40 | 50 | 60 | 70 | 80 | 90 | 100 |
|---|---|---|---|---|---|---|---|---|---|

Use gray or brown to color the shapes that have the numbers above.

61 15 48 22 100 20 60 11 30 90 43 10 50 80 77 62 70 40 69 25 45 83 64 92

On Safari

63

© Evan-Moor Corp. • EMC 8251 • Skill Sharpeners: Math

Page 64

Animal Toys

Skill: Determine the value of coins

Draw lines to match.

1¢ penny

5¢ nickel

8¢

12¢

10¢

15¢

On Safari

64

Skill Sharpeners: Math • EMC 8251 • © Evan-Moor Corp.

Page 65

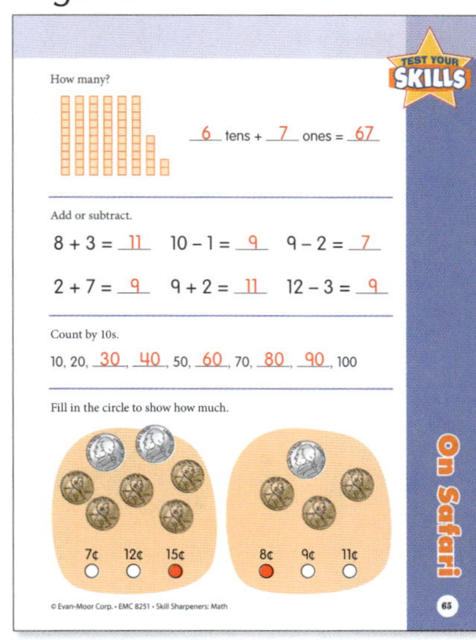
TEST YOUR SKILLS

How many?

6 tens + 7 ones = 67

Add or subtract.

8 + 3 = 11　10 − 1 = 9　9 − 2 = 7

2 + 7 = 9　9 + 2 = 11　12 − 3 = 9

Count by 10s.

10, 20, 30, 40, 50, 60, 70, 80, 90, 100

Fill in the circle to show how much.

7¢ 12¢ 15¢ (15¢ filled)

8¢ 9¢ 11¢ (8¢ filled)

On Safari

65

© Evan-Moor Corp. • EMC 8251 • Skill Sharpeners: Math

Page 66

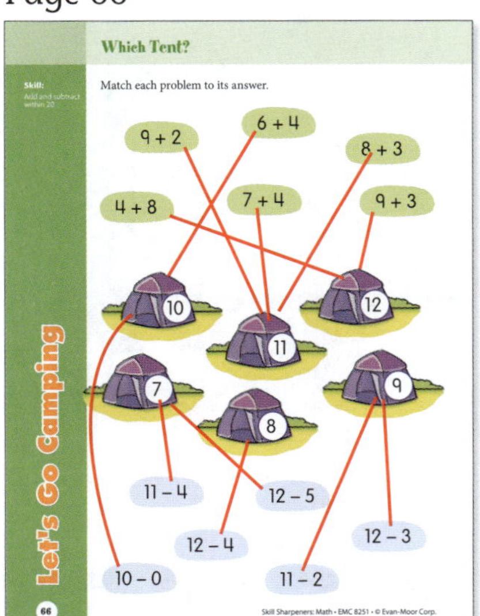
Which Tent?

Skill: Add and subtract within 20

Match each problem to its answer.

9 + 2　6 + 4　8 + 3　4 + 8　7 + 4　9 + 3

10　11　12　7　8　9

11 − 4　12 − 5　12 − 4　12 − 3　10 − 0　11 − 2

Let's Go Camping

66

Skill Sharpeners: Math • EMC 8251 • © Evan-Moor Corp.

Page 67

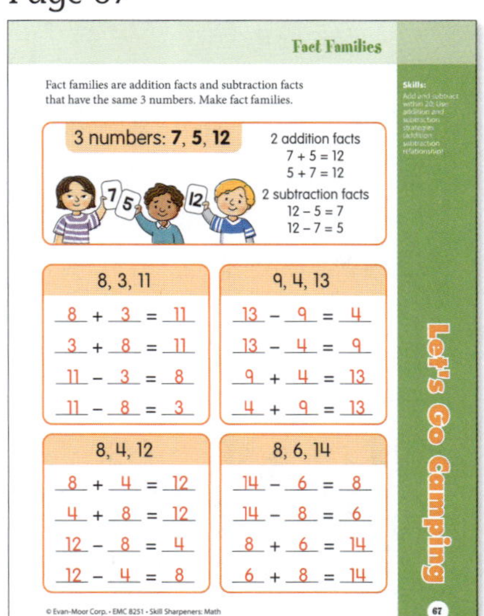
Fact Families

Skills: Add and subtract within 20. Use addition and subtraction strategies. Understand the addition-subtraction relationship.

Fact families are addition facts and subtraction facts that have the same 3 numbers. Make fact families.

3 numbers: 7, 5, 12

2 addition facts
7 + 5 = 12
5 + 7 = 12

2 subtraction facts
12 − 5 = 7
12 − 7 = 5

8, 3, 11
8 + 3 = 11
3 + 8 = 11
11 − 3 = 8
11 − 8 = 3

9, 4, 13
13 − 9 = 4
13 − 4 = 9
9 + 4 = 13
4 + 9 = 13

8, 4, 12
8 + 4 = 12
4 + 8 = 12
12 − 8 = 4
12 − 4 = 8

8, 6, 14
14 − 6 = 8
14 − 8 = 6
8 + 6 = 14
6 + 8 = 14

Let's Go Camping

67

© Evan-Moor Corp. • EMC 8251 • Skill Sharpeners: Math

Page 68

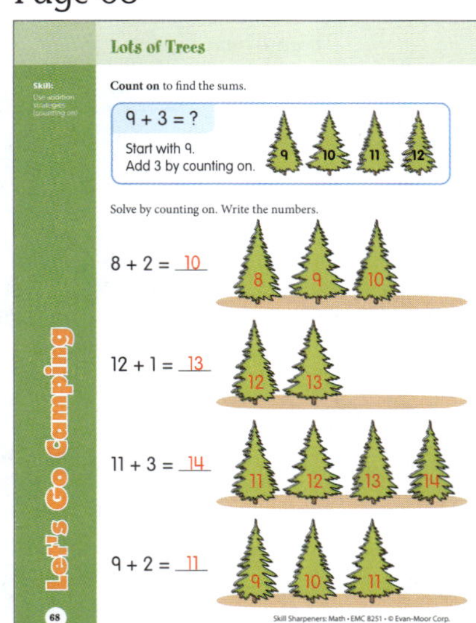
Lots of Trees

Skill: Use addition strategies (counting on)

Count on to find the sums.

9 + 3 = ?

Start with 9.
Add 3 by counting on.

9 10 11 12

Solve by counting on. Write the numbers.

8 + 2 = 10　(8, 9, 10)

12 + 1 = 13　(12, 13)

11 + 3 = 14　(11, 12, 13, 14)

9 + 2 = 11　(9, 10, 11)

Let's Go Camping

68

Skill Sharpeners: Math • EMC 8251 • © Evan-Moor Corp.

Page 69

Note: You may need to help your child read the word problems.

Busy Campers

Read. Solve the problems.

3 campers went fishing. 5 campers went swimming. 4 campers went hiking. How many campers were there?

12 campers

Raul is collecting leaves. He finds 4 red leaves, 3 orange leaves, and 7 yellow leaves. How many leaves did he find?

14 leaves

Kim, Candy, and Maria went fishing. Each girl caught 5 fish. How many fish did they catch in all?

15 fish

Tony saw birds at camp. He saw 7 jays, 3 hawks, and 4 quails. How many birds did he see?

14 birds

Write a word problem about this picture. Then write a number sentence for it.

Problems will vary.

5 + 7 + 2 = 14

Page 70

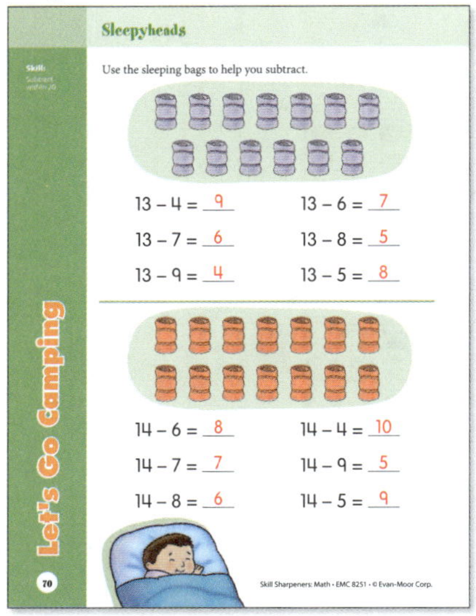

Sleepyheads

Use the sleeping bags to help you subtract.

13 – 4 = 9 | 13 – 6 = 7
13 – 7 = 6 | 13 – 8 = 5
13 – 9 = 4 | 13 – 5 = 8

14 – 6 = 8 | 14 – 4 = 10
14 – 7 = 7 | 14 – 9 = 5
14 – 8 = 6 | 14 – 5 = 9

Page 71

Note: You may need to help your child read the word problems.

A Week at Camp

Read. Solve the problems.

There were 13 scouts in Red Troop. 9 scouts went canoeing. The rest of the scouts went fishing. How many scouts went fishing?

4 scouts went fishing.

Gabe collected 14 leaves. He gave 5 leaves to a friend. How many leaves did Gabe have left?

Gabe had 9 leaves left.

Mary Anne toasted 8 marshmallows. Katie toasted 6 marshmallows. How many marshmallows were toasted in all?

14 marshmallows were toasted in all.

Blue Troop put up 12 tents. The wind blew down 8 tents. How many tents were still standing?

4 tents were still standing.

Page 72

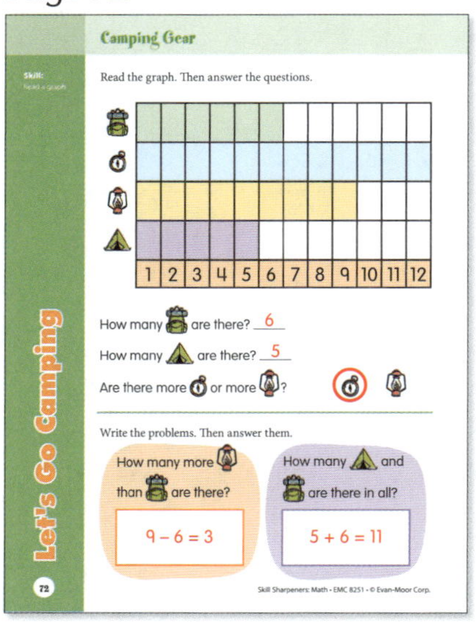

Camping Gear

Read the graph. Then answer the questions.

How many [backpack] are there? 6

How many [tent] are there? 5

Are there more [compass] or more [lantern]? [compass]

Write the problems. Then answer them.

How many more [lantern] than [backpack] are there? 9 – 6 = 3

How many [tent] and [backpack] are there in all? 5 + 6 = 11

Page 73

Through the Woods

This is a long path. Count by ones. Write the numbers.

51 52 53 54 55 56 57 58 59 60 61 62 63 64 65 66 67 68 69 70 71 72 73 74 75 76 77 78 79 80 81 82 83 84 85 86 87 88 89 90 91 92 93 94 95 96 97 98 99 100

Ten people sleep in each tent. Count by tens to find out how many people are sleeping.

10 20 30 40 50 60 70 80 90 100

Page 74

Before, After, or Between

Write the missing number.

70 71 72

| after | before | between |
|---|---|---|
| 21 22 | 46 47 | 29 30 31 |
| 39 40 | 49 50 | 43 44 45 |
| 45 46 | 35 36 | 38 39 40 |
| 50 51 | 63 64 | 51 52 53 |
| 64 65 | 20 21 | 67 68 69 |
| 77 78 | 91 92 | 80 81 82 |
| 99 100 | 62 63 | 87 88 89 |

Page 75

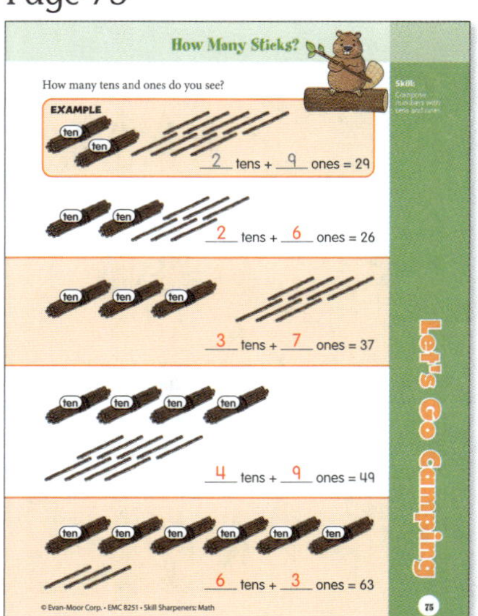

How Many Sticks?

How many tens and ones do you see?

EXAMPLE 2 tens + 9 ones = 29

2 tens + 6 ones = 26

3 tens + 7 ones = 37

4 tens + 9 ones = 49

6 tens + 3 ones = 63

Page 76

Comparing Fun

Write >, <, or =.

18 > 16 | 14 < 19 | 26 = 26
43 > 40 | 15 < 51 | 90 < 91
37 < 73 | 21 > 12 | 48 > 44
89 < 98 | 71 < 74 | 77 = 77

Answers will vary.

Write a number that is greater than 25. ____

Write a number that is less than 52. ____

Write a number that is equal to 99. 99

Page 77

More or Less

| 1 | 2 | 3 | 4 | 5 | 6 | 7 | 8 | 9 | 10 |
|---|---|---|---|---|---|---|---|---|---|
| 11 | 12 | 13 | 14 | 15 | 16 | 17 | 18 | 19 | 20 |
| 21 | 22 | 23 | 24 | 25 | 26 | 27 | 28 | 29 | 30 |
| 31 | 32 | 33 | 34 | 35 | 36 | 37 | 38 | 39 | 40 |
| 41 | 42 | 43 | 44 | 45 | 46 | 47 | 48 | 49 | 50 |
| 51 | 52 | 53 | 54 | 55 | 56 | 57 | 58 | 59 | 60 |
| 61 | 62 | 63 | 64 | 65 | 66 | 67 | 68 | 69 | 70 |
| 71 | 72 | 73 | 74 | 75 | 76 | 77 | 78 | 79 | 80 |
| 81 | 82 | 83 | 84 | 85 | 86 | 87 | 88 | 89 | 90 |
| 91 | 92 | 93 | 94 | 95 | 96 | 97 | 98 | 99 | 100 |

Write the missing numbers. Use the number chart to help you.

|  | 1 more | 1 less | 10 more | 10 less |
|---|---|---|---|---|
| 12 | 13 | 11 | 22 | 2 |
| 25 | 26 | 24 | 35 | 15 |
| 34 | 35 | 33 | 44 | 24 |
| 49 | 50 | 48 | 59 | 39 |
| 87 | 88 | 86 | 97 | 77 |

## Page 78

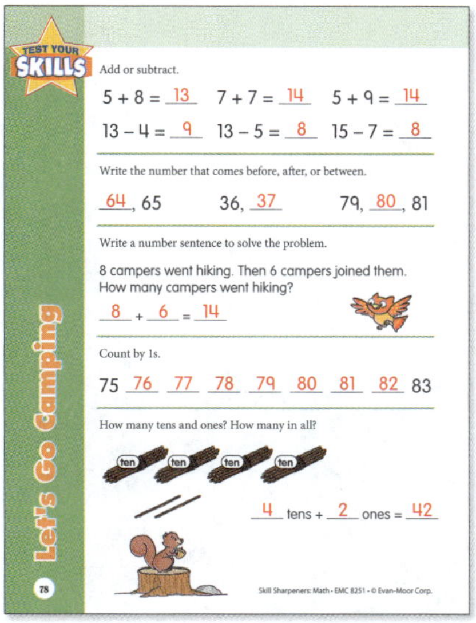

Test Your Skills

Add or subtract.

5 + 8 = 13 7 + 7 = 14 5 + 9 = 14

13 – 4 = 9 13 – 5 = 8 15 – 7 = 8

Write the number that comes before, after, or between.

64, 65 36, 37 79, 80, 81

Write a number sentence to solve the problem.

8 campers went hiking. Then 6 campers joined them. How many campers went hiking?

8 + 6 = 14

Count by 1s.

75 76 77 78 79 80 81 82 83

How many tens and ones? How many in all?

ten ten ten ten

4 tens + 2 ones = 42

Let's Go Camping

78 Skill Sharpeners: Math • EMC 8251 • © Evan-Moor Corp.

## Page 79

A Tasty Crop

Add or subtract. Then find the apples with answers that are the same as 3 + 3 + 3. Color those apples red. Color the other apples yellow.

Skill: Add and subtract within 20

7 + 8 = 15; 15 – 7 = 8; 15 – 8 = 7; 8 + 8 = 16; 16 – 8 = 8; 16 – 7 = 9; 8 + 7 = 15; 16 – 9 = 7; 15 – 6 = 9; 9 + 7 = 16; 6 + 9 = 15; 15 – 9 = 6

Fruity Fun

© Evan-Moor Corp. • EMC 8251 • Skill Sharpeners: Math 79

## Page 80

Fruity Facts

Skill: Add and subtract within 20

Add or subtract.

6 + 7 = 13 7 + 6 = 13 13 – 7 = 6 13 – 6 = 7

9 + 5 = 14 5 + 9 = 14 14 – 9 = 5 14 – 5 = 9

8 + 6 = 14 6 + 8 = 14 14 – 6 = 8 14 – 8 = 6

8 + 7 = 15 7 + 8 = 15 15 – 7 = 8 15 – 8 = 7

9 + 6 = 15 6 + 9 = 15 15 – 6 = 9 15 – 9 = 6

9 + 7 = 16 7 + 9 = 16 16 – 7 = 9 16 – 9 = 7

Fruity Fun

80 Skill Sharpeners: Math • EMC 8251 • © Evan-Moor Corp.

## Page 81

Note: You may need to help your child read the word problems.

What's Growing?

Read. Write the problems. Solve them.

Skills: Solve word problems; Add and subtract within 20

Dana planted 16 seeds. 7 seeds sprouted. How many seeds did not sprout? 9 seeds did not sprout. 16 – 7 = 9

Jamal picked 8 pears from a tree. Leah picked 7 pears from another tree. How many pears did they pick in all? They picked 15 pears. 8 + 7 = 15

A tree had 8 big plums and 8 little plums. How many plums were on the tree? There were 16 plums on the tree. 8 + 8 = 16

Kimi's tree had 15 apples. Ahmed's tree had 9 apples. How many more apples did Kimi's tree have than Ahmed's tree? Kimi's tree had 6 more apples. 15 – 9 = 6

Fruity Fun

© Evan-Moor Corp. • EMC 8251 • Skill Sharpeners: Math 81

## Page 82

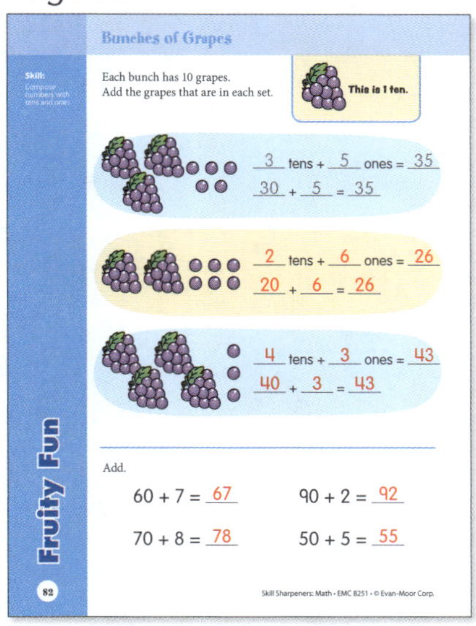

Bunches of Grapes

Skill: Compose numbers with tens and ones

Each bunch has 10 grapes. Add the grapes that are in each set.

This is 1 ten.

3 tens + 5 ones = 35 30 + 5 = 35

2 tens + 6 ones = 26 20 + 6 = 26

4 tens + 3 ones = 43 40 + 3 = 43

Add.

60 + 7 = 67 90 + 2 = 92

70 + 8 = 78 50 + 5 = 55

Fruity Fun

82 Skill Sharpeners: Math • EMC 8251 • © Evan-Moor Corp.

## Page 83

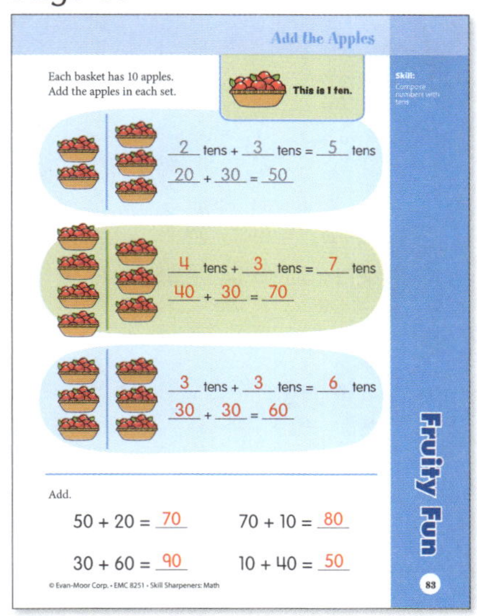

Add the Apples

Each basket has 10 apples. Add the apples in each set.

This is 1 ten.

Skill: Compose numbers with tens

2 tens + 3 tens = 5 tens 20 + 30 = 50

4 tens + 3 tens = 7 tens 40 + 30 = 70

3 tens + 3 tens = 6 tens 30 + 30 = 60

Add.

50 + 20 = 70 70 + 10 = 80

30 + 60 = 90 10 + 40 = 50

Fruity Fun

© Evan-Moor Corp. • EMC 8251 • Skill Sharpeners: Math 83

## Page 84

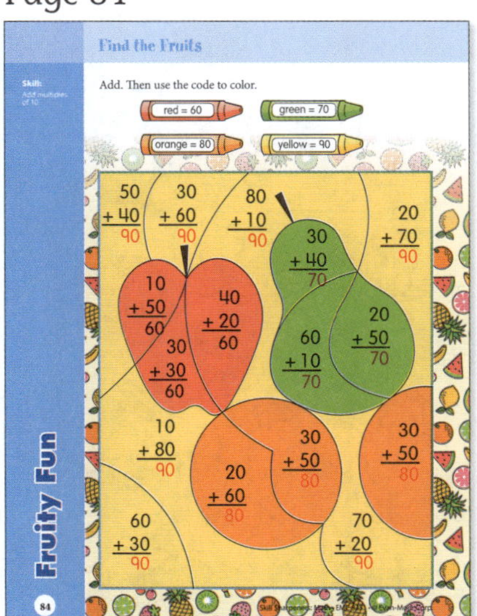

Find the Fruits

Skill: Add multiples of 10

Add. Then use the code to color.

red = 60 green = 70 orange = 80 yellow = 90

50 + 40 = 90; 30 + 60 = 90; 80 + 10 = 90; 30 + 40 = 70; 20 + 70 = 90; 10 + 50 = 60; 40 + 20 = 60; 20 + 50 = 70; 60 + 10 = 70; 30 + 30 = 60; 10 + 80 = 90; 30 + 50 = 80; 20 + 60 = 80; 30 + 50 = 80; 60 + 30 = 90; 70 + 20 = 90

Fruity Fun

84

## Page 85

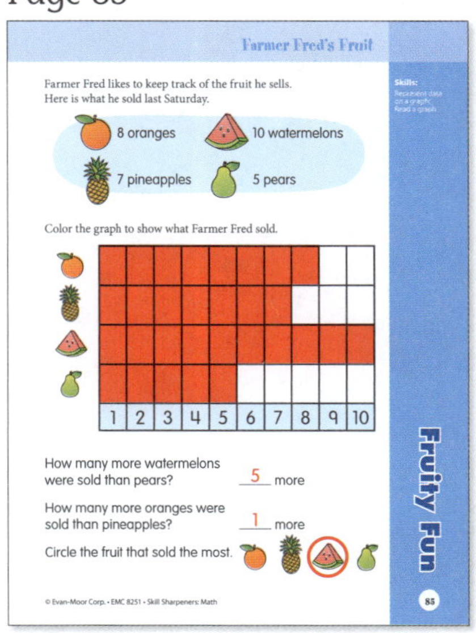

Farmer Fred's Fruit

Farmer Fred likes to keep track of the fruit he sells. Here is what he sold last Saturday.

Skills: Read and draw data on a graph; Read a graph

8 oranges 10 watermelons 7 pineapples 5 pears

Color the graph to show what Farmer Fred sold.

1 2 3 4 5 6 7 8 9 10

How many more watermelons were sold than pears? 5 more

How many more oranges were sold than pineapples? 1 more

Circle the fruit that sold the most.

Fruity Fun

© Evan-Moor Corp. • EMC 8251 • Skill Sharpeners: Math 85

## Page 86

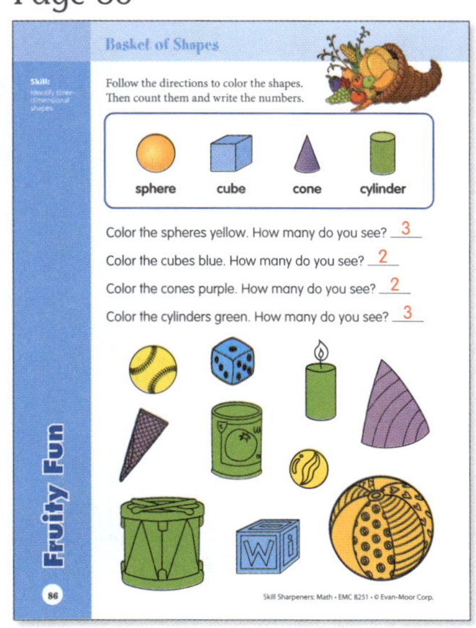

Basket of Shapes

Skill: Identify three-dimensional shapes

Follow the directions to color the shapes. Then count them and write the numbers.

sphere cube cone cylinder

Color the spheres yellow. How many do you see? 3

Color the cubes blue. How many do you see? 2

Color the cones purple. How many do you see? 2

Color the cylinders green. How many do you see? 3

Fruity Fun

86 Skill Sharpeners: Math • EMC 8251 • © Evan-Moor Corp.

Page 87

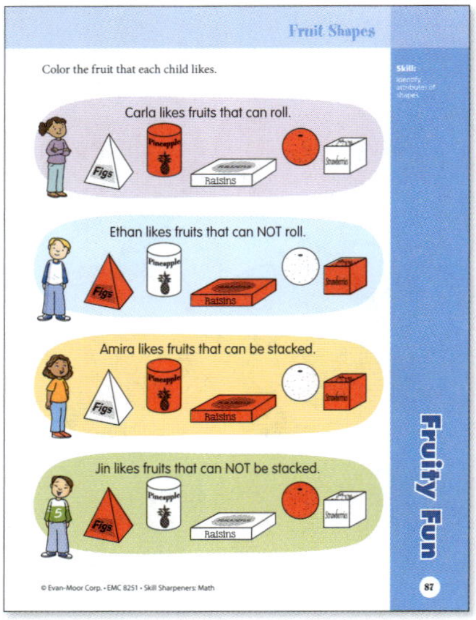
Fruit Shapes

Color the fruit that each child likes.

Carla likes fruits that can roll.

Ethan likes fruits that can NOT roll.

Amira likes fruits that can be stacked.

Jin likes fruits that can NOT be stacked.

Fruity Fun

87

Page 88

A Yummy Treat

Count by 5s.

5 10 15 20 25

30 35 40 45 50

Connect the dots.

Fruity Fun

88

Page 89

A Fruity Path

Count by 5s to get to the fruit trees.
Fill in the missing numbers.

5 10 15 20 25 30 35 40 45 50 55 60 65 70 75 80 85 90 95 100

Fruity Fun

89

Page 90

TEST YOUR SKILLS

Add or subtract.

7 + 8 = 15 16 – 8 = 8 15 – 6 = 9

9 + 7 = 16 15 – 7 = 8 16 – 9 = 7

Count by 5s.

5 10 15 20 25 30 35 40 45 50

55 60 65 70 75 80 85 90 95 100

Add.

4 tens + 2 tens = 6 tens

40 + 20 = 60

20 + 8 = 28 70 + 5 = 75

60 + 9 = 69 30 + 40 = 70

10 + 50 = 60 50 + 40 = 90

Fruity Fun

90

Page 91

Icy Homes

Add. Color the igloos with a sum of 17 yellow.
Color the igloos with a sum of 18 purple.

8 + 9 = 17

8 + 7 = 15

9 + 6 = 15

8 + 8 = 16 9 + 7 = 16

9 + 8 = 17

9 + 9 = 18 8 + 6 = 14

Chilly Capers

91

Page 92

Walrus Numbers

Use each set of numbers to make two addition problems and two subtraction problems.

| 8 6 14 | 7 8 15 |
|---|---|
| 8 + 6 = 14 | 7 + 8 = 15 |
| 6 + 8 = 14 | 8 + 7 = 15 |
| 14 – 8 = 6 | 15 – 7 = 8 |
| 14 – 6 = 8 | 15 – 8 = 7 |

| 9 7 16 | 8 9 17 |
|---|---|
| 9 + 7 = 16 | 8 + 9 = 17 |
| 7 + 9 = 16 | 9 + 8 = 17 |
| 16 – 9 = 7 | 17 – 8 = 9 |
| 16 – 7 = 9 | 17 – 9 = 8 |

Chilly Capers

92

Page 93

Polar Animals

Read. Write the problems. Solve them.

9 penguins were swimming in the sea. 8 more penguins jumped in. How many penguins were swimming in the sea then?

9 + 8 = 17

There were 17 penguins swimming in the sea then.

16 walruses were lying on the ice. 9 walruses slid back into the sea. How many walruses were still on the ice?

16 – 9 = 7

There were 7 walruses still on the ice.

Polar Bear saw 6 seals in the morning and 9 seals in the afternoon. How many seals did Polar Bear see that day?

6 + 9 = 15

Polar Bear saw 15 seals that day.

18 seals were playing in the water. 9 seals swam away. How many seals were still playing?

18 – 9 = 9

There were 9 seals still playing.

Chilly Capers

93

Page 94

Seeing Double

Add.

2 + 2 = 4; 3 + 3 = 6; 1 + 1 = 2; 5 + 5 = 10; 4 + 4 = 8; 6 + 6 = 12; 8 + 8 = 16; 7 + 7 = 14; 9 + 9 = 18; 10 + 10 = 20

Use the doubles addition facts to help you subtract.

12 – 6 = 6; 16 – 8 = 8; 18 – 9 = 9; 14 – 7 = 7

Chilly Capers

94

Page 95

Catch of the Day

Add.

EXAMPLE: 24 + 30 = 54

15 + 10 = 25; 24 + 20 = 44; 18 + 60 = 78; 27 + 20 = 47; 39 + 30 = 69; 27 + 40 = 67; 21 + 50 = 71; 16 + 70 = 86; 83 + 10 = 93; 52 + 30 = 82; 35 + 40 = 75

Chilly Capers

95

Page 96

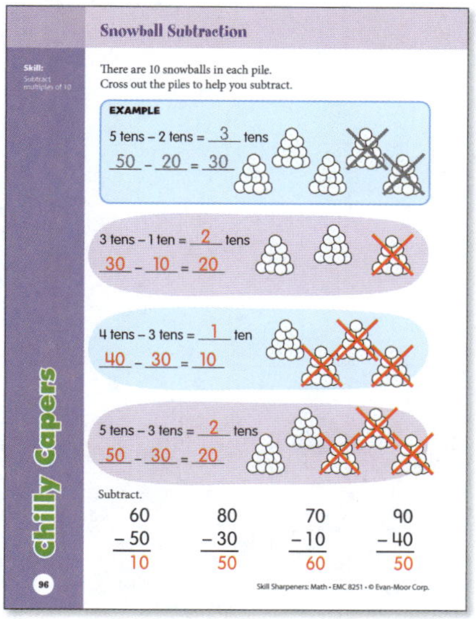
Snowball Subtraction

There are 10 snowballs in each pile.
Cross out the piles to help you subtract.

EXAMPLE
5 tens – 2 tens = 3 tens
50 – 20 = 30

3 tens – 1 ten = 2 tens
30 – 10 = 20

4 tens – 3 tens = 1 ten
40 – 30 = 10

5 tens – 3 tens = 2 tens
50 – 30 = 20

Subtract.
60 – 50 = 10
80 – 30 = 50
70 – 10 = 60
90 – 40 = 50

Page 97

Let It Snow!

Add or subtract.
15 + 30 = 45
20 + 60 = 80
82 – 20 = 62
60 + 30 = 90
90 – 20 = 70
70 – 50 = 20
40 + 40 = 80
60 – 30 = 30
30 + 40 = 70

Page 98

Winter Stickers

Add the coins. Write the price on the tag.
penny 1¢ nickel 5¢ dime 10¢
5¢ 12¢ 15¢ 22¢ 8¢ 16¢

Page 99

When Can We Go Sledding?

Write the time.
1:30 4:00 3:30
8:30 5:00 11:00
6:30 12:00 9:30

Page 100

How Many Fish?

Circle pairs of fish. Count by 2s. Write how many.
Circles will vary.
10 24 16 38

Count by 5s.
5, 10, 15, 20, 25, 30, 35, 40, 45, 50

Count by 10s.
10, 20, 30, 40, 50, 60, 70, 80, 90, 100

Page 101

Fun in the Snow

Count the mittens by 2s.
2 4 6 8 10
12 14 16 18 20

Count by 2s to slide down the hill.
2 4 6 8 10 12 14 16 18 20

Connect the dots. Color.

Page 102

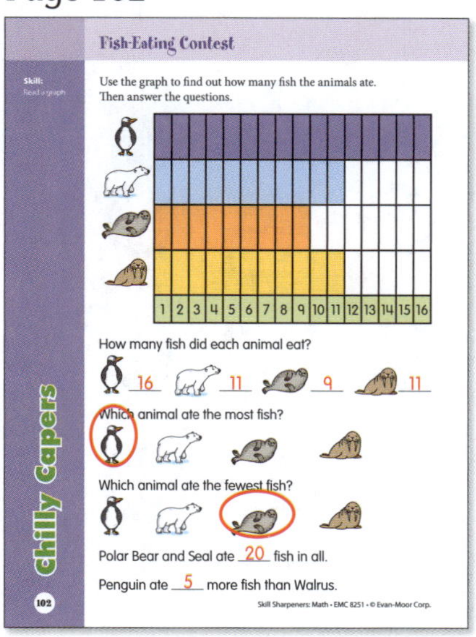
Fish-Eating Contest

Use the graph to find out how many fish the animals ate.
Then answer the questions.

How many fish did each animal eat?
16 11 9 11

Which animal ate the most fish?
Which animal ate the fewest fish?

Polar Bear and Seal ate 20 fish in all.
Penguin ate 5 more fish than Walrus.

Page 103

TEST YOUR SKILLS

Add or subtract.
8 + 9 = 17 9 + 9 = 18 9 + 8 = 17
17 – 9 = 8 17 – 8 = 9 18 – 9 = 9

Count by 2s.
2, 4, 6, 8, 10, 12, 14, 16, 18, 20

There were 9 gray seals and 8 brown seals.
How many seals were there?
9 + 8 = 17 There were 17 seals.

Add or subtract.
49 + 50 = 99
27 + 30 = 57
80 – 60 = 20
70 – 20 = 50

Write the time.
5:00 8:30

Page 104

Colorful Balloons

First add two numbers to make 10.
Then add the last number.
7 + 3 + 4 = 14
9 + 1 + 2 = 12
8 + 2 + 3 = 13
4 + 6 + 7 = 17
3 + 7 + 5 = 15
9 + 1 + 8 = 18
5 + 5 + 6 = 16
2 + 8 + 9 = 19
6 + 4 + 5 = 15

## Page 105

**Balls in the Air**

Circle the balls needed to make a group of 10. Then finish adding the rest.

**7 + 5 = ?**

7 + 3 = 10 10 + 2 = 12

**9 + 4 = ?**

9 + 1 = 10 10 + 3 = 13

**6 + 7 = ?**

6 + 4 = 10 10 + 3 = 13

**8 + 6 = ?**

8 + 2 = 10 10 + 4 = 14

At the Fair

## Page 106

**Number Carts**

Add.

6 + 7 = 13
8 + 6 = 14

9 + 9 = 18
5 + 7 = 12

9 + 8 = 17
5 + 9 = 14

8 + 8 = 16
6 + 9 = 15

Fill your own cart.

Answers will vary.

___ + ___ = ___
___ + ___ = ___

At the Fair

## Page 107

**A Roller Coaster Ride**

Add.

| | | | | |
|---|---|---|---|---|
| 46 + 30 = 76 | 20 + 30 = 50 | 70 + 8 = 78 | 51 + 40 = 91 | 73 + 20 = 93 |
| 36 + 60 = 96 | 50 + 30 = 80 | 80 + 9 = 89 | 42 + 40 = 82 | 15 + 40 = 55 |
| 17 + 60 = 77 | 12 + 80 = 92 | 29 + 20 = 49 | 10 + 50 = 60 | 20 + 50 = 70 |

At the Fair

## Page 108

**Tasty Treats**

Note: You may need to help your child read the word problems.

Read. Write the problems. Solve them.

Kai sold ice cream cones at the fair. He sold 35 cones before lunch. He sold 40 cones after lunch. How many ice cream cones did he sell at the fair?

35 + 40 = 75

Kai sold 75 ice cream cones.

Jason bought a bag of peanuts. There were 50 peanuts in the bag. Jason ate 20 peanuts. How many peanuts were left?

50 − 20 = 30

There were 30 peanuts left.

Anna sold 27 bags of popcorn. Sam sold 30 bags of popcorn. How many bags did they sell together?

27 + 30 = 57

They sold 57 bags of popcorn.

80 people bought cotton candy yesterday. 60 people bought cotton candy today. How many more people bought cotton candy yesterday than today?

80 − 60 = 20

20 more people bought cotton candy yesterday.

At the Fair

## Page 109

**Down We Go!**

Cross out tens to help you subtract.

54 − 20 = 34

38 − 20 = 18

42 − 10 = 32

57 − 40 = 17

69 − 30 = 39

At the Fair

## Page 110

**Cool Subtraction**

Subtract.

65 − 40 = 25
81 − 50 = 31
39 − 10 = 29
75 − 30 = 45
28 − 10 = 18
47 − 20 = 27
96 − 70 = 26
52 − 40 = 12
88 − 60 = 28
73 − 20 = 53

At the Fair

## Page 111

**Equal Parts**

How many equal parts are there?

4 parts 3 parts 1 part

6 parts 2 parts 4 parts

Which shapes have 2 **equal** parts? Circle them.

Which shapes have 4 **equal** parts? Circle them.

At the Fair

## Page 112

**Fraction Fun**

Color one half of each shape green. Answers will vary.

Color one fourth of each shape blue. Answers will vary.

Draw a line to make 2 equal parts. Color one half green.

Draw lines to make 4 equal parts. Color one fourth blue.

Answers will vary.

At the Fair

## Page 113

**When Will They Go?**

Six families are going to the fair at different times. Draw lines to match the clocks.

2:00 9:00 11:30 8:30 10:30 12:00

Jones family — 2:00
Eng family — 11:30
Lee family — 10:30
Santos family — 9:00
Sidhu family — 8:30
Miller family — 12:00

At the Fair

## Page 114

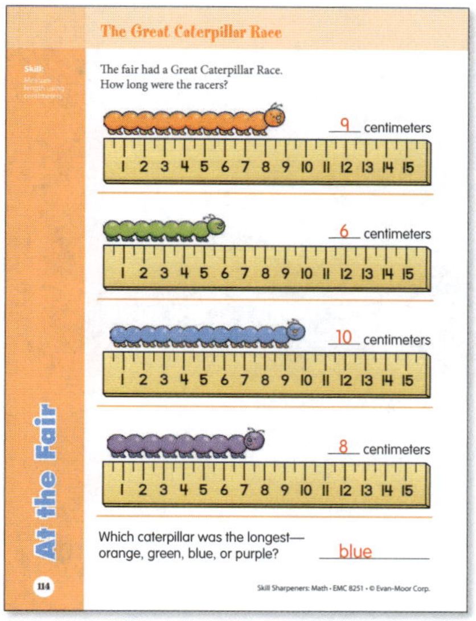
The Great Caterpillar Race

Skill: Measure length using centimeters

The fair had a Great Caterpillar Race. How long were the racers?

9 centimeters

6 centimeters

10 centimeters

8 centimeters

Which caterpillar was the longest—orange, green, blue, or purple? blue

At the Fair

114 Skill Sharpeners: Math • EMC 8251 • © Evan-Moor Corp.

## Page 115

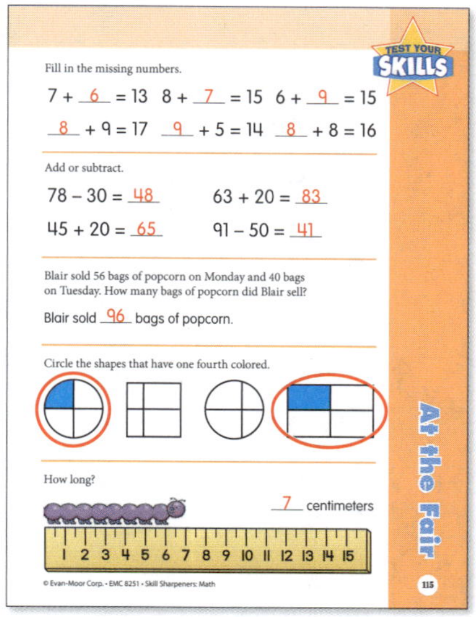
Test Your Skills

Fill in the missing numbers.

7 + 6 = 13   8 + 7 = 15   6 + 9 = 15

8 + 9 = 17   9 + 5 = 14   8 + 8 = 16

Add or subtract.

78 – 30 = 48   63 + 20 = 83

45 + 20 = 65   91 – 50 = 41

Blair sold 56 bags of popcorn on Monday and 40 bags on Tuesday. How many bags of popcorn did Blair sell?

Blair sold 96 bags of popcorn.

Circle the shapes that have one fourth colored.

How long?

7 centimeters

At the Fair

© Evan-Moor Corp. • EMC 8251 • Skill Sharpeners: Math 115

## Page 116

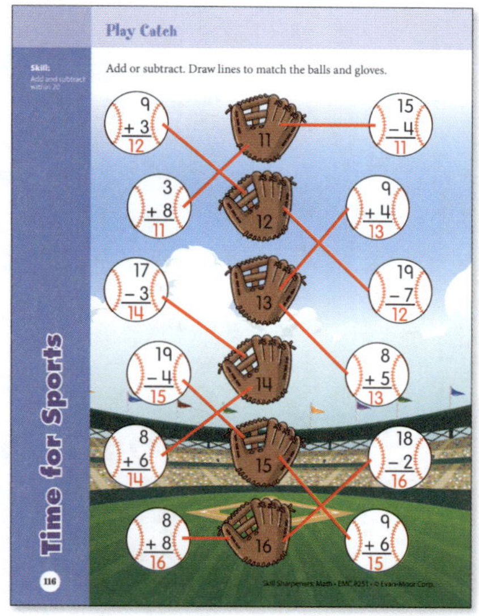
Play Catch

Skill: Add and subtract within 20

Add or subtract. Draw lines to match the balls and gloves.

9 + 3 = 12; 15 – 4 = 11; 3 + 8 = 11; 9 + 4 = 13; 17 – 3 = 14; 19 – 7 = 12; 19 – 4 = 15; 8 + 5 = 13; 8 + 6 = 14; 18 – 2 = 16; 8 + 8 = 16; 9 + 6 = 15

Gloves: 11, 12, 13, 14, 15, 16

Time for Sports

116 Skill Sharpeners: Math • EMC 8251 • © Evan-Moor Corp.

## Page 117

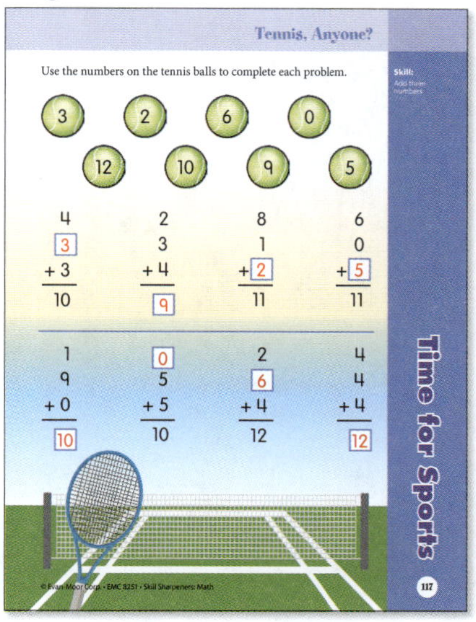
Tennis, Anyone?

Skill: Add three numbers

Use the numbers on the tennis balls to complete each problem.

3 2 6 0 12 10 9 5

4 + 3 + 3 = 10; 2 + 3 + 4 = 9; 8 + 1 + 2 = 11; 6 + 0 + 5 = 11

1 + 9 + 0 = 10; 0 + 5 + 5 = 10; 2 + 6 + 4 = 12; 4 + 4 + 4 = 12

Time for Sports

© Evan-Moor Corp. • EMC 8251 • Skill Sharpeners: Math 117

## Page 118

Let's Bowl

Skill: Sequence two-digit numbers

Write the numbers in order from the least to the greatest.

EXAMPLE: 15 5 50 → 5 15 50

43 14 34 → 14 34 43

76 67 77 → 67 76 77

19 99 90 → 19 90 99

80 85 58 → 58 80 85

Bowling

Time for Sports

118 Skill Sharpeners: Math • EMC 8251 • © Evan-Moor Corp.

## Page 119

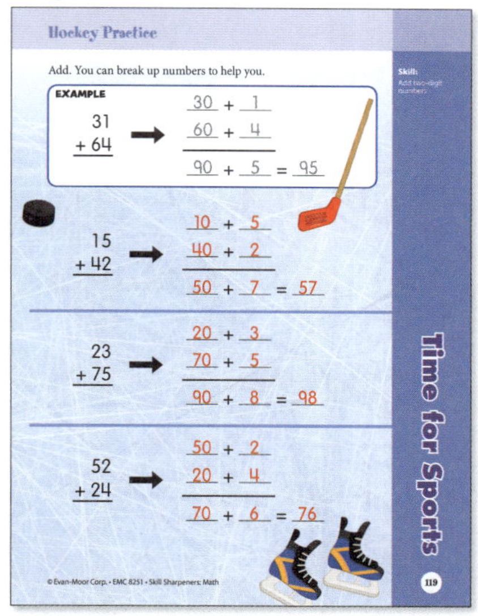
Hockey Practice

Skill: Add two-digit numbers

Add. You can break up numbers to help you.

EXAMPLE: 31 + 64 → 30 + 1, 60 + 4, 90 + 5 = 95

15 + 42 → 10 + 5, 40 + 2, 50 + 7 = 57

23 + 75 → 20 + 3, 70 + 5, 90 + 8 = 98

52 + 24 → 50 + 2, 20 + 4, 70 + 6 = 76

Time for Sports

© Evan-Moor Corp. • EMC 8251 • Skill Sharpeners: Math 119

## Page 120

A Great Shot

Skill: Add and subtract two-digit numbers

Add or subtract the ones first. Then add or subtract the tens.

27 + 30 = 57 (start on the ones side); 98 – 25 = 73; 13 + 31 = 44

64 – 30 = 34; 60 + 25 = 85; 37 – 27 = 10

86 – 75 = 11; 71 – 51 = 20; 51 + 44 = 95

Time for Sports

120 Skill Sharpeners: Math • EMC 8251 • © Evan-Moor Corp.

## Page 121

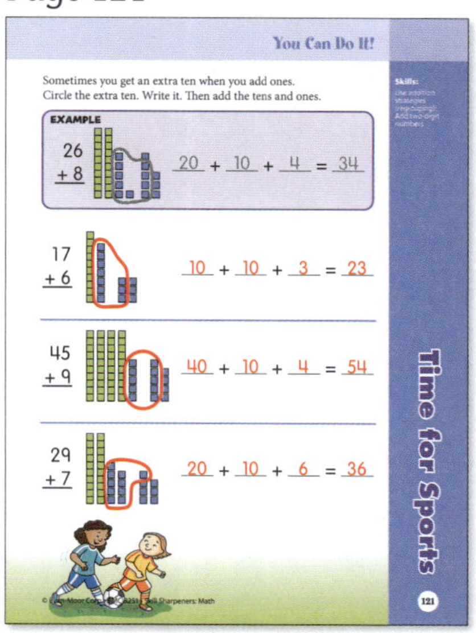
You Can Do It!

Skills: Use addition strategies (regrouping); Add two-digit numbers

Sometimes you get an extra ten when you add ones. Circle the extra ten. Write it. Then add the tens and ones.

EXAMPLE: 26 + 8 → 20 + 10 + 4 = 34

17 + 6 → 10 + 10 + 3 = 23

45 + 9 → 40 + 10 + 4 = 54

29 + 7 → 20 + 10 + 6 = 36

Time for Sports

© Evan-Moor Corp. • EMC 8251 • Skill Sharpeners: Math 121

## Page 122

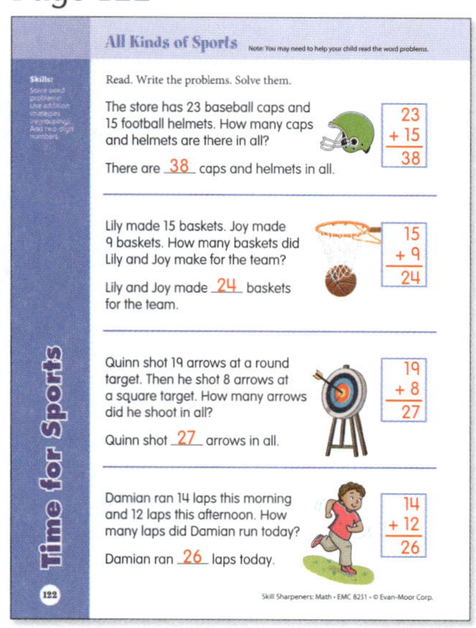
All Kinds of Sports

Note: You may need to help your child read the word problems.

Skills: Solve word problems; Use addition strategies (regrouping); Add two-digit numbers

Read. Write the problems. Solve them.

The store has 23 baseball caps and 15 football helmets. How many caps and helmets are there in all? 23 + 15 = 38

There are 38 caps and helmets in all.

Lily made 15 baskets. Joy made 9 baskets. How many baskets did Lily and Joy make for the team? 15 + 9 = 24

Lily and Joy made 24 baskets for the team.

Quinn shot 19 arrows at a round target. Then he shot 8 arrows at a square target. How many arrows did he shoot in all? 19 + 8 = 27

Quinn shot 27 arrows in all.

Damian ran 14 laps this morning and 12 laps this afternoon. How many laps did Damian run today? 14 + 12 = 26

Damian ran 26 laps today.

Time for Sports

122 Skill Sharpeners: Math • EMC 8251 • © Evan-Moor Corp.

## Page 123

### Off to the Game

Help the family get to the sports stadium. Count by 5s to 100. Write the numbers on the road.

Skill: Count by 5s

5, 10, 15, 20, 25, 30, 35, 40, 45, 50, 55, 60, 65, 70, 75, 80, 85, 90, 95, 100

STADIUM

Time for Sports

© Evan-Moor Corp. • EMC 8251 • Skill Sharpeners: Math

123

## Page 124

### Let the Games Begin!

Skill: Tell time to the half hour

Write the time that each game will start.

Soccer Game 2 : 00

Baseball Game 6 : 30

Hockey Game 7 : 30

Basketball Game 4 : 00

Draw hands on the clock to show when each game starts.

Golf Game 12:00

Tennis Match 9:00

Time for Sports

124

Skill Sharpeners: Math • EMC 8251 • © Evan-Moor Corp.

## Page 125

### Basketball Schedule

Skill: Read a data table

Dylan, Kelly, Mia, and Lin will play basketball today. The table shows when their teams will practice.

| Practice Schedule | |
|---|---|
| Dylan's Team | 1:00 |
| Kelly's Team | 1:30 |
| Mia's Team | 2:30 |
| Lin's Team | 4:00 |

Use the table to answer the questions.

Who will play basketball first? Dylan

Who will practice at 2:30? Mia

What time is the last practice? 4:00

Who will practice after Mia? Lin

What time will Kelly practice? 1:30

Will Mia start before or after 3:00? before

Time for Sports

© Evan-Moor Corp. • EMC 8251 • Skill Sharpeners: Math

125

## Page 126

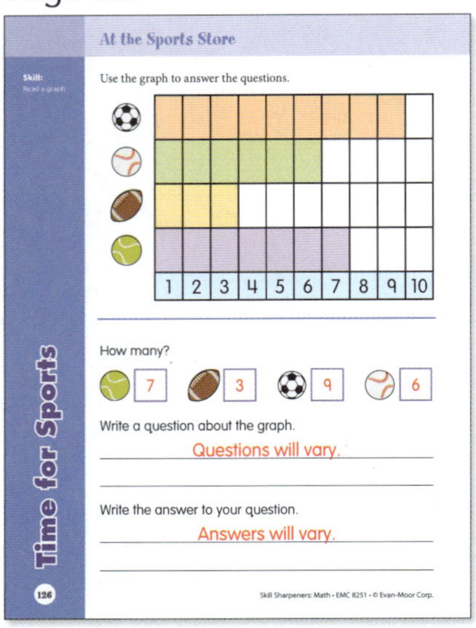

### At the Sports Store

Skill: Read a graph

Use the graph to answer the questions.

1 2 3 4 5 6 7 8 9 10

How many? 7 3 9 6

Write a question about the graph.

Questions will vary.

Write the answer to your question.

Answers will vary.

Time for Sports

126

Skill Sharpeners: Math • EMC 8251 • © Evan-Moor Corp.

## Page 127

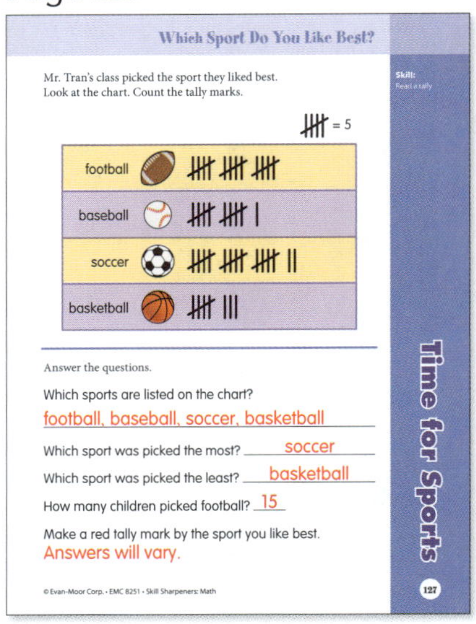

### Which Sport Do You Like Best?

Skill: Read a tally

Mr. Tran's class picked the sport they liked best. Look at the chart. Count the tally marks.

卌 = 5

football, baseball, soccer, basketball

Answer the questions.

Which sports are listed on the chart? football, baseball, soccer, basketball

Which sport was picked the most? soccer

Which sport was picked the least? basketball

How many children picked football? 15

Make a red tally mark by the sport you like best.
Answers will vary.

Time for Sports

© Evan-Moor Corp. • EMC 8251 • Skill Sharpeners: Math

127

## Page 128

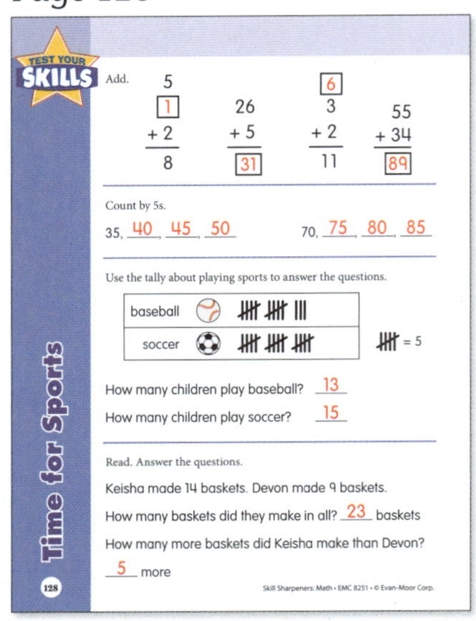

TEST YOUR SKILLS

Add.

5 + 1 + 2 = 8

26 + 5 = 31

6 + 3 + 2 = 11

55 + 34 = 89

Count by 5s.

35, 40, 45, 50

70, 75, 80, 85

Use the tally about playing sports to answer the questions.

baseball, soccer

卌 = 5

How many children play baseball? 13

How many children play soccer? 15

Read. Answer the questions.

Keisha made 14 baskets. Devon made 9 baskets.

How many baskets did they make in all? 23 baskets

How many more baskets did Keisha make than Devon?

5 more

Time for Sports

128

Skill Sharpeners: Math • EMC 8251 • © Evan-Moor Corp.